T0108774

TORN IN TWO

TORN
IN TWO

THE SINKING OF THE *DANIEL J. MORRELL*
AND ONE MAN'S SURVIVAL ON THE OPEN SEA

MICHAEL SCHUMACHER

UNIVERSITY OF MINNESOTA PRESS
MINNEAPOLIS ◆ LONDON

Published by the University of Minnesota Press
111 Third Avenue South, Suite 290
Minneapolis, MN 55401-2520
http://www.upress.umn.edu

Printed in the United States of America on acid-free paper

The University of Minnesota is an equal-opportunity educator and employer.

22 21 20 19 18 17 16   10 9 8 7 6 5 4 3 2 1

Library of Congress Cataloging-in-Publication Data
Names: Schumacher, Michael, author.
Title: Torn in two : the sinking of the *Daniel J. Morrell* and one man's
    survival on the open sea / Michael Schumacher.
Description: Minneapolis : University of Minnesota Press, [2016] | Includes
    index. Identifiers: LCCN 2016019427 (print) | ISBN 978-0-8166-9521-8 (hc)
Subjects: LCSH: *Daniel J. Morrell* (Ship) | Shipwrecks—Huron, Lake (Mich. and
    Ont.) | Hale, Dennis. | Shipwreck victims—Huron, Lake (Mich. and Ont.) |
    Shipwreck survival—Huron, Lake (Mich. and Ont.) | Huron, Lake (Mich. and
    Ont.)—History—20th century.
Classification: LCC G530.D252 (print) | DDC 917.7404/43—dc23
LC record available at https://lccn.loc.gov/2016019427

For Dennis Hale
and those who lost their lives on the *Daniel J. Morrell*

CONTENTS

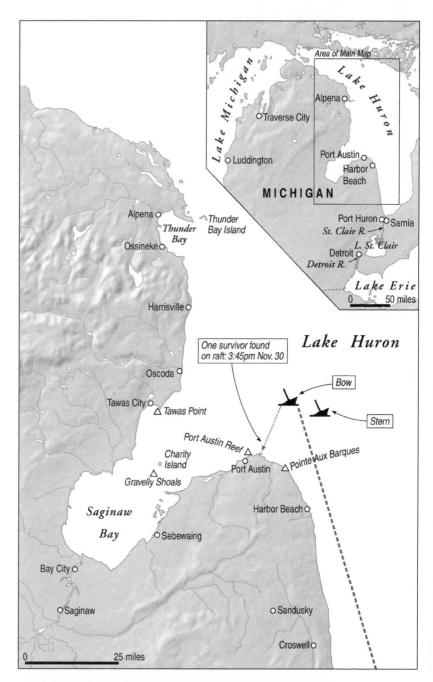

After being torn in two, the *Daniel J. Morrell* sank northwest of Pointe Aux Barques on the night of November 29, 1966. The Coast Guard recovered the ship's only survivor, Dennis Hale, more than thirty-six hours later. Map by Philip Schwartzberg, Meridian Mapping, Minneapolis.

PROLOGUE
CARELESSNESS AND FATE

D ENNIS HALE PULLED HIS CAR INTO THE BETHLEHEM STEEL plant just in time to see the *Daniel J. Morrell* reaching the Buffalo breakwater on Lake Erie, a short distance from the plant's Lackawanna loading dock. It was eleven in the evening of November 26, 1966. Hale, a twenty-six-year-old watchman on the bulk carrier, had missed the boat—quite literally—on other occasions, but never with so much riding on it. If he failed to make this last trip of the season, he would be forfeiting his annual bonus, vacation pay, and extended vacation pay, adding up to a loss of six to seven thousand dollars.

Seeing the boat's lights in the near distance only added to Hale's growing frustrations over recent developments on the *Morrell*. He had not been home for Thanksgiving because he was working on what was scheduled to be the *Morrell*'s last trip of the season. He could have accepted this as part of the downside of working on the lakes late in the season, but when the *Morrell* was sailing on the return trip to Lackawanna, New York, a port near Buffalo, the boat's master, Captain Arthur Crawley, learned that the *Morrell* would be required to return to Taconite Harbor, Minnesota, for yet another load; the Bethlehem Steel freighter slated for the trip had engine problems. The *Morrell*, along with her sister ship, the *Edward Y. Townsend*, would be substituting for the stricken vessel. The additional voyage would be the *Morrell*'s thirty-fourth run of the shipping season.

There was no reason, other than carelessness and bad timing, for Hale's not being on the boat. When the *Morrell* had arrived at Lackawanna, she could not immediately unload. Two freighters were ahead of her at the dock. Hale viewed this inconvenience as an unexpected opportunity: his Ashtabula, Ohio, home was only three hours away, and since it took nearly eight hours to unload the average freighter, he estimated that he could drive home, see his wife and spend the night in his own bed, and return to Lackawanna in plenty of time to be back onboard the *Morrell* before she sailed for Minnesota. Hale kept his car at the Bethlehem plant for occasions like this.

Hale left as soon as he found someone to cover his watch duty. John Groh, a twenty-one-year-old deckwatch on the *Morrell*, hitched a ride with him. Groh resided in Erie, Pennsylvania, which was not out of the way, and Hale dropped him off before driving on to Ashtabula.

Hale, it turned out, miscalculated how long it would take to unload the boats—and Captain Crawley's determination to leave the docks as soon as possible. The Lackawanna–Taconite trip was a long but familiar haul, one that the crew on the *Morrell* had taken on many occasions. This one promised to be a little rougher than most. Weather forecasts called for stormy weather on Lake Erie, and Captain Crawley ordered water added to the *Morrell*'s ballast tanks. The extra weight would allow the *Morrell* to ride lower in the water, giving her better stability. The smallest and shallowest of the Great Lakes, Lake Erie was notorious for the ferocity of its late-autumn storms.

As soon as they knew that they were stranded, Hale and Groh visited the Coast Guard station and radioed Crawley. With any luck, they could find a way to hook up with the boat on her first stop of the trip. Hale told the captain that his car had broken down on his way to Lackawanna, a transparently bad excuse that Crawley probably saw through. Nevertheless, Crawley had little choice but to accommodate the two tardy crewmen. Already short-handed in his crew, Crawley wanted the two onboard. The *Morrell*, he told them, would be taking on a load of coal the next day at Mullen Dock, near Windsor, Ontario. Hale and Groh could rejoin the crew at that time.

Hale assured him that he would be there.

The *Daniel J. Morrell* enters Lake Huron around 11:00 a.m. on November 25, 1966. This view by Thomas Sykora is one of the last photographs taken of the ore carrier. Kenneth Thro Collection, University of Wisconsin–Superior.

SEASON OF THE WITCH

OFFICIALS AT THE CAMBRIA STEAMSHIP COMPANY HAD GOOD reason to celebrate in 1906, when the *Daniel J. Morrell* and *Edward Y. Townsend* began their service as two of the longest and sturdiest bulk carriers on the Great Lakes. Times were good and the demand for iron ore high. New vessels were being constructed at a brisk pace. At the time of her launch on August 18, the *Townsend*, at 602 feet, was longer than any boat on the lakes. The *Morrell*, launched four days later, was 1 foot shorter.

Six-hundred-foot freighters spelled the future of Great Lakes commercial shipping. Earlier in 1906, on April 26, the *J. Pierpont Morgan* became the "Queen of the Lakes," a term applied to the lengthiest boat working on the Great Lakes. The *Henry H. Rogers*, launched on June 16, measured the same, as did the *Norman B. Ream* and the *Peter A. B. Widener*, launched later that same year. These vessels set the standard for all that would follow.

As author, Great Lakes historian, and former sailor Mark L. Thompson notes in his book *Queen of the Lakes*, these behemoths were more economical than their smaller predecessors, and not simply because they could haul greater cargoes. They could be built quickly and, on a ton-for-ton basis, more economically than the other steamers, which meant that they could be out on the lakes, earning money for their owners, in less time than others. "The standard 600-footer was the first 'economy model,'" Thompson writes. Boats like the *Morrell* and *Townsend*, he concludes, were "the backbone of the world's most efficient bulk shipping industry."

They could not have arrived at a more opportune time. The discovery of the Mesabi Iron Range forty years earlier, coupled with the other vast iron ore deposits in Minnesota, had increased demand for shipping to steel firms around the Great Lakes, leading to windfall profits, the

Built to haul enormous cargo tonnage to ports all around the Great Lakes, the *Morrell* was one of only a handful of 600-foot freighters at the time of her launching in 1906. Lake Superior Maritime Collection, University of Wisconsin–Superior Special Collections.

development and expansion of the railroad system, and the construction and improvement of greater dockside facilities. The old wooden boats and schooners, once the mainstays in commercial shipping, were disappearing, replaced by steel, steam-driven freighters capable of hauling greater loads with less dependence upon wind and weather conditions. Even the shape of the vessels was changing. At one time, the pilothouse was located in the middle of the boat, with hatches located in front and back of it; a new design, with the wheelhouse located forward and the engine room and another deckhouse located aft, left the middle of these elongated boats open for uninterrupted hatches and cargo holds, making cargo loading, storage, and unloading more efficient. The first of this new design, the *R. J. Hackett*, the brainchild of Cleveland shipbuilder Eli Peck, checked in at a very modest 211 feet, but boat lengths increased in all the new vessels that followed. The design would last for more than a century.

Other than paint, the first of the 600-footers were very similar. All had 58-foot beams, and all were within a few feet of each other in length.

The *Edward Y. Townsend*, the *Morrell*'s sister ship, takes on cargo at the dock in Ashtabula, Ohio, in this early undated photograph. Courtesy of Michael Rozzo.

All were equipped with triple-expansion, coal-burning engines generating 1,800 horsepower. All carried cargoes of about 11,000 tons.

The mid-to-late-1800s saw great expansion in the steel business, including the 1862 founding of the Cambria Iron Company in Johnstown, Pennsylvania. As operators of the largest rail mill in the United States, Cambria had a vested interest in shipping iron to its plant, and the Cambria Steamship Company, based in Cleveland, became a subsidiary created to accomplish that. Cambria Iron Company reorganized and changed its name to Cambria Iron Works in 1898. Ten years later—two years after the launching of the *Daniel J. Morrell* and *Edward Y. Townsend*—Cambria Iron Works came under the management of the M. A. Hanna Company. In 1923, Bethlehem Steel would purchase Cambria.

Oddly enough, the *Morrell* and *Townsend* were considered sister ships, even though they were constructed by different shipbuilders, the *Morrell* by West Bay Shipbuilding in West Bay, Michigan, the *Townsend* by Superior Shipbuilding in Superior, Wisconsin. The sister ship designation probably arose from the fact that they were identical, operating for the same company, and launched within a month of each other in 1906. Both had been named for executives who worked for Cambria Iron Works.

Daniel J. Morrell (1821–1885), the *Morrell*'s namesake, had been an influential, powerful businessman and politician in his day. Born in Maine, he had moved to Philadelphia when he was fifteen, before moving to Johnstown, Pennsylvania, in 1855, where he took the job as general superintendent and manager of the Cambria Iron Company. He also served as the president of a bank and as president of the Johnstown gas and water company. His years as a public servant included a long stint as president of the Johnstown City Council and two terms as a Republican congressman in Washington D.C.

Edward Y. Townsend (1824–1891) had been similarly involved with the Cambria Iron Company. After spending his early adult years working for Wood, Abbott, & Co., a Philadelphia-based dry goods firm serving the southern and western portions of the United States, and earning a reputation as a first-rate businessman, Townsend wound up with the Cambria Iron Company, eventually serving as the company's president from 1873 until his death in 1891. He saw devastating events during his tenure with Cambria, first when the company's rolling mill was destroyed by a fire, and then in 1889, when the Johnstown Flood took the lives of many of his friends and workers at Cambria and destroyed the plant itself. He worked

Daniel J. Morrell, general superintendent and manager of the Cambria Iron Company, member of the U.S. House of Representatives, and namesake of the ill-fated ore boat. Brady–Handy Photograph Collection, Library of Congress Prints and Photographs Division.

tirelessly on restoring operations at the plant. According to his *New York Times* obituary, the flood gave Townsend "a shock from which he never fully recovered."

Neither of the men lived to see the construction of their namesakes.

The *Daniel J. Morrell*'s six decades of service on the Great Lakes were very productive and, for the most part, uneventful. She carried huge loads, as expected, and occasionally set tonnage records for the cargo poured down

An early view of the *Daniel J. Morrell* under steam. Detroit Publishing Company Photograph Collection, Library of Congress Prints and Photographs Division.

The *Morrell* unloads cargo under the Huletts at a Lake Erie port. The Fr. Edward J. Dowling, S.J., Marine Historical Collection, University of Detroit Mercy.

her eighteen hatches. She experienced some trouble with her compass in her early years, but she had only one noteworthy mishap, when in 1909 she collided with the *Henry Phipps*, another 600-footer, at Whitefish Point, Michigan. The damage was extensive, but both boats returned to service.

There were the usual improvements over the years. In 1922, the *Morrell* made history when she became the first bulk carrier on the Great Lakes to use a gyrocompass. In 1956, a new 3,200-horsepower Skinner engine was installed, nearly doubling the boat's horsepower. The *Morrell* might have been a half-century old at that point, but Bethlehem Steel, managing the *Morrell* since 1930, saw a future for the ore carrier.

When the Coast Guard inspected the *Morrell* prior to the 1966 shipping season, the inspectors saw a venerable, hard-working vessel beginning to show her age. She was seaworthy, but any boat with that many years of service had suffered some physical indignities from all the loading and unloading, the twisting and bending in heavy seas, and general day-to-day operations. The fall seasons had taken an invisible toll as well: the steel used in shipbuilding prior to 1948 could become weakened and brittle when sailing in cold, stormy weather. There had to be flexibility in the hull, of course, or a vessel would just snap in two in such weather conditions, but there was also the issue of accumulative weakening over time, not unlike the way a paper clip, bent back and forth repeatedly, will eventually weaken and break.

No one onboard the *Morrell* could have gauged—or even suspected—the condition of the boat's hull when she left Lackawanna for her last trip of the 1966 season, but the storm on Lake Huron was about to offer the ultimate test of her strength.

➤ ➤ ➤

The *Morrell* faced deteriorating weather conditions as she sailed west across Lake Erie and then north on the Detroit River. Wind velocity was increasing, creating waves that strained the *Morrell*'s riveted hull. Rather than sail through the night in adverse conditions, Captain Crawley decided to drop anchor below Detroit and see where the weather stood the following morning. He called the Bethlehem Steel dispatcher in Cleveland at six in the evening and reported his decision.

The *Morrell*'s forty-seven-year-old master had only been with the boat for three months, and this probably influenced his decision. This was his first serious fall storm since taking command of the *Morrell,* and he was still learning how she handled in rough weather. In fact, this was Crawley's first season as a master of any vessel. He had had his master's papers for years, but he had never used them. A native of Cleveland, presently living in Rocky River, Ohio, Crawley had been working on bulk carriers since his graduation from high school, but the lifelong bachelor found it a lonely calling. He was assigned his first command earlier in the year, when he became captain of the *Lebanon,* which, ironically, was the very first freighter he had worked on twenty-nine years earlier. He had taken over the *Morrell* when her captain retired in the midst of the 1966 season.

No captain, regardless of his experience, would deliberately risk his vessel and crew by recklessly sailing in dangerous conditions, and late-season storms on the Great Lakes demanded extra caution. Less than a decade earlier, in 1958, the *Carl D. Bradley,* a bulk carrier bigger and newer than the *Morrell,* had broken in two and sunk on Lake Michigan; only two of her crew had survived, and only then under extraordinary circumstances.

The *Edward Y. Townsend* had departed the Lackawanna dock four hours after the *Morrell,* and at 11:10 p.m., five hours after the *Morrell* dropped anchor in the Detroit River, Captain Thomas J. Connelly saw the *Morrell* and radioed Captain Crawley. The *Townsend* had taken a pounding in the storm, but Connelly intended to continue north and anchor near Stag Island in the upper St. Clair River.

Dennis Hale, of course, knew none of this when he and John Groh set out for Windsor the following morning. He had talked a friend into driving them in his (Hale's) car, and when they arrived at the Windsor dock at eleven that morning, the *Morrell* was nowhere to be seen—nor would she be in sight for the next sixteen hours. Captain Crawley, respecting the high winds in the Detroit area, had kept the *Morrell* anchored for thirteen hours. While waiting for the *Morrell's* arrival, Hale and Groh idled their hours around the docks, cadging a meal in the galley of another boat and catching some sleep in the fuel dock's locker room.

The *Morrell* finally pulled into port, loaded 221 tons of coal, and left Windsor. The wind, while freshening, was not yet threatening, but Captain Crawley continued to be concerned about what he was seeing from the pilothouse windows and what he was hearing on the weather reports. Although the wind on Lake Huron was estimated between six and eighteen miles per hour at the time of the *Morrell's* departure from the coal docks, the Weather Bureau forecast issued from Chicago called for gale conditions

Watchman Dennis Hale can be seen at the bow of the *Morrell* as the ship moves through the St. Clair River in 1965. Father Peter Van der Linden collection; courtesy of John Belliveau.

for the northern third of Lake Huron, and heavy sailing conditions for the rest of the lake. The *Morrell* had faced as much—and worse—during her six decades of service on the Great Lakes. Just eight years earlier, while sailing under similar ballasted conditions, the *Morrell* had been lashed by a vicious November storm. Her wires shrieked in one-hundred-miles-per-hour winds, and according to William C. Hull, the *Morrell's* second mate at the time, she had plowed through twenty-five-foot seas.

One could speculate that Captain Crawley might have stayed anchored had this not been his last trip of the season. He had options to consider when he made his decision to sail. If the storm proved to be too much, he could find shelter, drop anchor, and wait it out. Otherwise he would proceed cautiously and hope that the bad weather would pass over the next day. It didn't hurt, either, that the predicted winds would be coming out of the north or northwest for much of the haul up Lake Huron. Crawley would be taking the *Morrell* directly into the storm, as opposed to having heavy seas hitting the boat from behind. If need be, the *Morrell* could hug Michigan's eastern shore, sheltering her from seas that might build up from winds out of the west.

> > >

The Witch of November: A storm could brew on the Great Lakes at almost any time, but the eleventh month of the year was the month feared most by sailors. Storms on the Great Lakes were especially violent during these thirty days, when temperatures were in flux and cold air masses from the north passed over water still warm from summer. A boat could leave port and sail on glassy water, only to face life-threatening sailing conditions a few hours later when an unexpected storm blew in. Doppler radar, GPS systems, computerized storm projections, and other scientific and technological advances taken for granted today did not exist in the mid- or even late twentieth century; jet streams were yet to be discovered in the early part of the century, when the jet itself was decades away.

In *Queen of the Lakes*, Mark L. Thompson calls November "the archenemy of countless generations of sailors who have crewed the big freighters":

The mood on the ore boats changes markedly when the calendars are turned over to November. A heavy pall of apprehension descends on the ships, mirroring the blanket of dirty grey clouds that covers the lakes throughout most of the month. Tempers grow short, and patience is a scarce commodity. Consumption of alcohol goes up, and, in the privacy of their rooms, crewmembers who normally scoff at the frequent lifesaving drills hang their lifejackets and survival suits where they can get at them in a hurry. It's not an issue of whether there will be a storm in November, only a question of when it comes. And it's likely that there will be more than one.

Weather reporting was sketchy, especially in the first half of the century. The U.S. Weather Bureau in Washington, D.C., tried to keep ports around the Great Lakes as informed and up-to-date as possible, but its projections in the first half of the twentieth century were based on a time-consuming process. Information about weather conditions was collected from Great Lakes weather reporting stations, and weather maps were drawn up, but all too often by the time the data and projections were sent to ports around the lakes, the weather had changed. Mariners tended to be skeptical. With November weather being as volatile as it was, an ore boat's captain had to rely on instinct and experience as much as on the storm postings and dated weather information.

The captain always had the final say whether to sail or stay in, but a number of factors entered the decision about sailing in November, especially near the end of the month, when the shipping season was drawing to a close. At one time, captains received tonnage bonuses for their annual hauls, and they stood to earn bigger bonuses if they took their vessels out for a couple of runs at the end of the season. On other occasions, such as the *Morrell*'s, a captain might be ordered to make a trip or two to satisfy a company's tonnage projections for a given season. The captains' dispositions entered into the decisions, as well. The more cautious masters kept their vessels off the lakes when the weather got rough. Others, known as "heavy-weather captains," supremely confident in their boats' abilities, would not hesitate to go out when the winds were whipping up and the waves were building.

The captains of the *Daniel J. Morrell* and *Edward Y. Townsend* faced a rare, if not unique, situation when making their decisions to sail: not only did both work for the same company, but both boats were almost identical in structure, destined for the same port, sailing in the same conditions on the same lake. It would have been very strange if one sailed and the other stayed in. Both captains had considerable experience on the lakes. Captain Thomas Connelly had spent twenty-seven of his forty-eight years on the lakes, while Arthur Crowley had been working on the water for two years longer. They were well acquainted with Lake Huron.

But storms, as both men knew, had a way of testing a master's knowledge and experience. Much newer vessels, mastered by more experienced captains, had been lost in monster storms that had become legend in the shipping trade. In 1905, over the last three days of November, a storm ripped through Minnesota and settled on Lake Superior, wrecking or stranding dozens of vessels and barges, and claiming the lives of twenty-eight men, including nine on the *Mataafa*, a 430-foot freighter that split and lay stranded at the entry to the Duluth port. While hundreds of spectators huddled onshore in subzero temperatures, nine men trapped on the back of the boat slowly froze to death. Maritime historian William Ratigan, in his seminal study *Great Lakes Shipwrecks & Survivals*, refers to the storm as "a hurricane [that] ripped the world of fresh water apart."

In 1940, a rapidly moving storm system tore through Minnesota and on to Lakes Superior, Michigan, and Huron on Armistice Day, taking the lives of 49 in Minnesota and 150 throughout the Midwest. Much of the destruction was on inland lakes, where the storm caught many duck hunters by surprise. The weather had been uncommonly warm, and the hunters and others were caught unprepared for the plunging temperatures and precipitation that went from rain to sleet to ice to blizzard snow. Seventy-miles-per-hour winds raked the area, whipping up enormous waves on the smaller lakes, as well as on Lake Superior. Hunters out on small islands, unable to escape in their boats, were trapped and froze to death. Others drowned when their boats capsized.

Lake Michigan took the worst of it. On that lake alone, three freighters were sunk, and dozens of other vessels were grounded, pounded mercilessly, or blown off course. On Lake Huron it was much the same; two ore carriers met their demise, while a dozen boats were grounded. In all, sixty-six sailors lost their lives on the lakes during the storm.

Lake Michigan was also the setting for the loss of the largest vessel to sink on the Great Lakes to that point, when the *Carl D. Bradley* broke in two and sank on November 15, 1958, taking thirty-three men to their deaths. In her day, the 638-foot limestone carrier, launched in 1927 and based out of Rogers City, Michigan, had the reputation of being one of the strongest boats on the lakes. She set tonnage records hauling stone from the limestone quarry near Rogers City to steel mills around the Great Lakes, where the stone was used in the iron purification process. On her final trip, the *Bradley* had dropped off a load of stone near Gary, Indiana, and was headed back, under ballast, to Rogers City, when she was caught in a ferocious storm on Lake Michigan. She was working well in the storm's sixty- to sixty-five-miles-per-hour winds and thirty-foot waves when, with no warning whatsoever, she suddenly began to tear apart. She sank in a matter of minutes. Four of the crew managed to climb aboard a life raft. The other thirty-one officers and crew members found themselves trapped in the boat or plunged into icy water, where they drowned or died of hypothermia.

What followed became one of the most remarkable survival stories in

Great Lakes history. The *Bradley* sank as the late-fall darkness was setting in, at about 5:30 p.m., and for the next fifteen hours, the survivors hung on, despite being tossed back in the lake when waves flipped the raft. One died of exposure. The others fought to stay alive in subfreezing temperatures and howling winds. Two men, forty-three-year-old first mate Elmer Fleming and twenty-six-year-old deck watchman Frank Mays, survived and were rescued by the Coast Guard. The other, twenty-one-year-old watchman Gary Strzeleki, jumped overboard early in the morning when he thought he had seen land and decided to make a swim for it; he died shortly after being picked up by the Coast Guard.

These and other storms held places in Great Lakes maritime lore, but they paled in comparison to the massive storm that settled over all five lakes over a four-day period in 1913. No storm in Great Lakes history could equal the death and destruction caused by this "white water hurricane," occurring between Thursday, November 7, and Monday, November 10. In a four- to six-hour period on November 10, eight freighters were lost, with all hands, on Lake Huron. All told, more than 250 sailors perished aboard vessels on Lakes Superior, Michigan, Huron, and Erie.

The storm formed when a weak low pressure system from the southwest joined a stronger low pressure "clipper" system originating in the Arctic and eventually running along the United States–Canadian border, dipping down into Minnesota and on to Lake Superior and Lake Michigan. Gale warnings were posted in ports around Lake Superior, but many captains went out anyway. The storm brought higher wind velocity than anticipated. It attacked any boat that dared to be out on Lake Superior. Two vessels, the *Leafield*, a British-built package freighter carrying a cargo of steel rods, and the 525-foot *Henry B. Smith*, carrying a load of iron ore, were lost, along with forty-three men. Eight other boats were grounded, with three men lost on one when they attempted to launch a lifeboat and seek assistance for their stranded vessel. One of the grounded boats, the *L. C. Waldo*, had her rudder torn off while she fought through gigantic waves in a desperate attempt to reach the safety of the Keweenaw Peninsula.

On Lake Michigan, seven men lost their lives on the *Plymouth*, a barge that sank after a tug pulling her towed her to an island and cut her loose. The *Louisiana*, a wooden boat built in 1887, grounded near Washington Island, Wisconsin, caught fire and burned to the waterline. Further down the lake, waves heavily damaged breakwater construction in Milwaukee and washed away a project extending Chicago's Lincoln Park.

As it turned out, this was only the beginning. By Sunday morning, November 9, the storm seemed to be blowing itself out. Lake Huron was calm. Freighter captains, after taking a cautious approach and keeping their boats in while the storm raged on the two upper Great Lakes, left loading docks and ports, and took their freighters out on Lake Huron. What they did not know was that the original storm front from the upper Great Lakes, while weakening, was combining with a very powerful front racing in from the nation's southeast, creating a storm of epic proportion. The system blew in so quickly that captains, after smooth sailing early in the day, found themselves in life-threatening conditions with almost no warning. One churchgoer near Point Clark, attending midmorning services, was amazed by the ferocity and sudden appearance of the storm. "The lake was calm as glass," he said of Lake Huron at the time when he walked through the doors of his church. "By the time church was over, it was obvious that no boat could be safe in the water."

The storm was deadly in Michigan and all across the Ohio valley. In Cleveland, a wintry mix of rain and slushy snow became a blizzard that paralyzed the city for days. On Lake Huron, the barometer dropped to record-low readings; blizzard snows brought visibility down to a point where vessels were essentially sailing blind; thick ice formed on decks, making it very hazardous to walk forward to aft on the boats.

What those surviving time on Lake Huron that day would remember was the wind. Gale force to hurricane force winds punished the vessels relentlessly, pushing boats off course, driving them onshore or onto shoals, trapping them in troughs, and threatening to flip them over. The strongest and newest of the bulk carriers were as abused as the older ones. One freighter, the *Charles S. Price*, a three-year-old, 524-foot straight-decker, turned turtle in the southern portion of the lake and was discovered upside down, with only a small portion of her bow floating above water; twenty-eight men lost their lives. The brand-new *James Carruthers*, a veteran of two trips in her career on the lakes and equipped with all the safety features of the day, vanished with her crew of twenty-two. On Lake Erie, *Lightship 82*, a floating lighthouse stationed near Buffalo, was torn from its moorings, and, without power, cast to waves that overwhelmed her and her crew of six.

The extent of the damage and the sheer number of lives lost were uncertain until bodies and wreckage drifted to shore over the following days. The heaviest loss was on Lake Huron. Eight freighters sank with all hands.

The *Daniel J. Morrell* was photographed on the St. Clair River around 5:00 p.m. on November 25, 1966, just days before her sinking. Photograph by Emory Massman. Kenneth Thro Collection, University of Wisconsin–Superior.

Although exact crew lists were not kept in those days, roughly two hundred sailors perished. Of all the upbound boats on Lake Huron on November 9, only one reached its final destination on time.

The storm the *Daniel J. Morrell*, *Edward Y. Townsend*, and other boats on Lake Huron now faced was taking on the characteristics and dimensions of some of the historical storms on the Great Lakes. November 1966 had been a study in contrasts in Michigan. The beginning and end of the month had been unseasonably cold, with greater than average precipitation, contributing to a record amount of snowfall for the month. The middle of the month had been warm and mild, as if Indian summer had decided to pay the state a second visit.

The cold snap of the last week of November was especially brutal. When arctic air made its way south and met the lingering warm air Michiganers had been enjoying, protracted stormy weather set in, lasting the better part of a week. The Upper Peninsula took the brunt of it. Blizzard conditions stranded more than two hundred cars, many returning home after the Thanksgiving holiday. Sixty-miles-per-hour winds brought down trees and power lines. Half of the homes in Marquette lost their power. Faye and Leslie Purman, owners of a lodge catering to sportsmen, died after closing the lodge for the winter and getting stuck in snow on their drive home; they apparently decided to walk for help, about four and a half miles away, but never made it. Their bodies would be found on December 1.

The storm punched its way to the south, bringing high winds and heavy snow. It showed no sign of relenting. The *Daniel J. Morrell* and *Edward Y. Townsend* had sailed the storm's outer region when they moved across Lake Erie and into the rivers leading to Lake Huron.

The new day—November 28—would find them sailing into the teeth of it.

❯ ❯ ❯

Dennis Hale took a fair amount of good-natured verbal abuse when he boarded the *Morrell* in Ontario, his crewmates wondering if the woman he had undoubtedly seen had been worth the money he would be losing for the hours he had missed during his absence on the early portion of the trip.

Hale shrugged it off. This was part of the typical camaraderie among shipmates on a typical Great Lakes freighter. Hale knew, all too well, that he would have been handing out the same kind of ribbing had he and one of his tormentors been in the opposite positions.

Although it was inevitable that some crew members might not care for others, it was essential that they work as a team. The engine crew tended to hang out together, their work bonding them; the same could be said about the deck crew or those working in the galley. The officers maintained a professional distance from the men they commanded, though the best made a point of keeping things as casual as possible, especially when they were off duty. An eight- or nine-month shipping season could be very long if you were unhappy with the men alongside you.

The crew quarters on the *Daniel J. Morrell*, like those on most ore boats, were located near the crewmen's work stations. The engine room and galley were located in the stern section of the boat; the engineers, oilers, firemen, coal passers, cooks, and porters had rooms in the aft housing. The forward quarters were occupied by the officers, wheelsmen, watchmen, and deckhands. On this trip, Hale was lucky enough to have a cabin to himself.

Each crewman worked two four-hour shifts per day. Hale worked the 4:00 a.m. to 8:00 a.m., and 4:00 p.m. to 8:00 p.m. shifts, and since the

Morrell pulled away from the dock at 7:30 on the morning of November 28, he had only a half hour ahead of him. Another watchman volunteered to take the final thirty minutes of Hale's shift. Hale appreciated the gesture. With the winds increasing and a forecast calling for rain or snow, it was going to be miserable standing watch on the deck.

Hale's job found him not only watching for other vessels but also working on general maintenance. This was hardly backbreaking work for a six-foot, 220-pound man. Although he had a wife, two children, and two stepchildren in Ashtabula, the *Morrell* was like a true family to Hale. He and his wife, Bertha, had been through some rough marital patches over the months, and he found life on the lakes a soothing respite, especially when he was trying to smooth over problems at home.

Hale headed to the galley as soon as the *Morrell* set out for Lake Huron. He grabbed some chicken for a couple of shipmates, delivered it, and talked about the weather with Stu Campbell, the *Morrell's* sixty-year-old wheelsman, now in the pilothouse. The weather was getting worse, but Campbell assured him that everything was going to be just fine.

Hale retreated to his room. He had eight hours before his next watch. He figured to pick at Carl Sandburg's *Lincoln*—a book his sister recommended, which he found to be too dry for his tastes—and then catch up on his sleep.

❯ ❯ ❯

The sailing on Lake Huron got rougher with each passing hour. The *Morrell* and *Townsend* were heading straight into the storm, struggling against heavy winds that shifted direction without warning from out of the north to northeast to northwest. The Weather Bureau forecast had warned of gale conditions, though the sailing in the lower part of Lake Huron had been relatively smooth. Captains Crawley and Connelly had conferred when the *Townsend* was heading out at about three o'clock in the afternoon and the sailing looked promising. The two masters were keeping a close watch on the conditions farther up the lake, but they saw nothing to be too concerned about—yet. The wind was freshening and the waves building, but the boats were handling it well.

The weather deteriorated in the hours ahead. The waves, by Connelly's estimation, were twelve feet at ten o'clock; an hour and a half earlier, when he had spoken to Crawley, they measured eight feet. Now the waves were building in heavy winds exceeding fifty miles per hour, and were coming at them from two directions at once. Blizzard snow fell around them. The boats could barely move forward in seas that seemed to be pushing them back. Both boats were rolling.

Captains Crawley and Connelly needed all their expertise just to keep their vessels on course. At ten o'clock, when the two spoke over the radio-phone, the *Townsend* was about eight miles north of Harbor Beach, near the tip of lower Michigan's thumb, the *Morrell* somewhere about fifteen miles north of her. The two men talked about the weather's potential. Connelly, worried about the possibility of his boat's broaching and being trapped in deadly troughs, restricted all movement between the forward and aft sections of his boat for the next twenty-four hours; anyone out on deck risked being washed overboard. Connelly was still satisfied with the way the *Townsend* was handling the storm, but he was beginning to wonder whether he should seek shelter in Thunder Bay.

By midnight, the *Morrell* and *Townsend* were taking tremendous punishment in the storm. Waves surged beneath the boats, coming in at 250- to 300-foot intervals between crests, resulting in more than one wave being beneath the boats at one time. The two freighters' sixty-year-old hulls twisted from all the action. Rivets sheared off from the twisting. Anchors slammed off their housings on the sides of the bows. Gigantic seas lifted the boats' sterns out of the water, causing an overspinning of the propellers and forcing the engineers to check down the propellers' rpms, lest the boat suffer an additional beating when the sterns slammed back down in the water and unchecked propellers sent shivers down the length of the vessels.

The captains stayed in contact throughout the later part of the evening. Neither boat seemed to be doing any better than the other. Connelly told Crawley that he was thinking about packing it in for the night. He had a choice of directing his boat to Thunder Bay, as he had been considering for a couple of hours, or turning the *Townsend* around and making a run for Port Huron. Connelly favored the Thunder Bay option. Retreating to Port Huron was risky. Turning his vessel around in such seas meant exposing her midships to direct hits from the waves, which might be enough to capsize it. James Van Buskirk, captain of the freighter *Benson Ford*, listening in on his radio to a conversation between Crawley and Connelly, cut into their communication. He had passed Thunder Bay, he told them, and he could vouch for the safety it would provide them. Buskirk would later tell the Coast Guard that he felt that the two captains intended to navigate their boats to the bay.

Just before midnight, Crawley contacted Connelly again. Connelly stated that he would have to call back, that he was tied up in the pilot-house. The *Townsend* was being blown off course and was broaching in violent seas. When Connelly returned the call at 12:15 a.m., he learned that Crawley was having similar problems. Although he gave no indication of his position, Crawley mentioned that he, too, was being blown off course. The conversation was very brief. The two men wished each other well and returned to their duties.

They would never speak to each other again.

The loss of the *Daniel J. Morrell* was front-page news throughout the Great Lakes states.

LOST

D ENNIS HALE WAS AWAKENED FROM A SOUND SLEEP BY A LOUD bang, which he initially shrugged off as the sound of an anchor pounding off the boat's bow in the storm. He rolled over, hoping to resume his sleep. A second bang was accompanied by the sound of his books falling off their shelf in a sudden avalanche. Hale reached for his light, but it didn't work. He yanked his curtain aside and sat up, just as the *Morrell's* general alarm sounded. Hale jumped to his feet and groped around in the darkness for the life jacket stowed on a rack above his bed. He slipped it on and, clad only in his boxer shorts, headed out of his cabin.

In the darkened causeway, he ran into Al Whoeme, a fifty-one-year-old deckwatch. They rushed together to the opening to the spar deck, Whoeme in the lead.

"Oh my God!" Whoeme shouted when he saw the cause for the alarm. He turned around and sprinted back in the direction of his room. He would be needing a life jacket.

Hale was similarly astonished when he stepped onto the spar deck and looked back toward the stern of the *Morrell*—or what should have been the back of the boat. The massive deck of the *Morrell*, with its eighteen cargo hatches, was longer than a football field, and behind the deck was the after housing, with its distinct black smokestack. From where he stood, Hale could not see the back half of the *Morrell*. Even the smokestack had disappeared. After a few seconds, the stern section rose into view. Unlike the bow portion, which was totally dark, the stern, including running lights, was still under complete power. The boat, Hale realized, had cracked at the keel and was breaking apart.

The *Daniel J. Morrell* breaking apart in heavy seas. Illustration by Robert McGreevy. Kenneth Thro Collection, University of Wisconsin–Superior.

The storm raged on, with no sign of letting up. Gigantic waves sent spray and water over the *Morrell's* rails. The wind created a cacophony of deafening sounds. Snow had turned to slush on the boat's deck.

"She broke in two from the bottom up," Hale would remember. "I could hear tearing metal, steam escaping, the wind in the wires, the engine laboring. She tore real slow, like a piece of paper. I could see sparks flying from it."

Hale hurried back to his cabin. He needed more clothing if he expected to have a chance of surviving after the *Morrell* sank. But in the blackness and his sense of urgency, he couldn't locate his clothes. He found his heavy peacoat and pulled it over his life jacket. This would have to do. For all he knew, the freighter would slip beneath the waves before he reached the life raft.

The *Morrell's* forward raft was located between the third and fourth hatches. Men were now gathering on it or standing nearby, some tying themselves to the raft so they wouldn't be swept overboard by the waves. The pontoon-style raft, constructed with a deck of two-by-fours mounted on large metal barrels, was set up to float free when the vessel sank. It supposedly held fifteen men, though it was difficult to imagine that many sailors fitting in the limited deck space for any extended period of time. Only minutes had passed since the initial sounding of the general alarm, yet in that time almost all of the officers and crew from the forward section of the *Morrell* had made their way to the raft.

No one panicked. If anything, the crewmen were remarkably calm, transfixed by what they were observing in the middle of the boat. Huge waves rolling under the *Morrell* lifted the breaking center portion of the boat high in the air, tearing it further before slamming it back down when a wave passed. Rivets popped from the twisting and tearing. The friction sent sparks into the night. The noise from the boat and the storm was ear-shattering.

Incredibly, no one at the back of the boat seemed to be aware of what was happening. With the engine running as normal, the stern was still under full power. The general alarm, cut off when the wiring was severed when the *Morrell* began to break up, was not sounding. The two lifeboats sat unattended in their davits.

To those aboard the life raft, the splitting of the *Morrell* seemed to take forever, though she actually broke apart in a few minutes. Captain Crawley, among those seated on the raft, informed the others that the pilothouse had lost power before anyone could transmit an SOS. He was only able to set off the general alarm by battery. The *Morrell*, he confessed, should not have been out in this storm, which turned out to be much worse than he anticipated. Other boats were in the area—including the *Townsend*, which he calculated to be roughly fifteen miles behind the *Morrell*—and while none of the men on board the other vessels knew of the *Morrell*'s plight, they could be alerted by using the parachute flares stowed on the life raft.

Don Worcester, one of the *Morrell*'s oilers, stepped out of one of the after cabins, holding an oil can and staring forward at the front of the boat. He gave no indication of recognizing what was happening in the middle of the boat. It was possible that someone in the engine room suspected that something serious had occurred and had sent him to the deck, but he was in no hurry to return to his station.

The *Morrell* finally split into two pieces. Without power or the ability to direct her course, the bow section was tossed about by seas that were now topping at twenty-five feet or better. A wintry mix of icy rain and snow pelted the men on the raft. All they could do was hold on and wait for the inevitable. It would not be long. Water flooded into the split-open cargo hold, weighing down the torn forward section from the back, lifting the boat's bow high in the air.

The stern portion of the *Morrell* was an entirely different story. Still under power and holding an even keel in the water, the gigantic aft section had become a battering ram, slamming into the bow, driving it forward, then slamming it again. The stern worked its way to the side of the bow until it was almost perpendicular to the other half. The two sections separated, the bow, pushed by the waves, drifting away. Then, to the horror of those on the raft, the stern made a run toward the bow. From where they sat, the men on the raft could see deep into the cargo hold of the vessel now charging toward them. Since they were low in the water, they were in danger of being crushed if the stern section rode over the bow's deck.

"From my perch on the raft I was staring into the open maw of the cargo hold," Hale would recall. "The clouds of steam swirling around the cargo lights were a glimpse of hell, and I felt I was looking into the gaping mouth of a monster that was about to devour me."

A mountainous wave washed over the deck, dislodged the life raft, and threw everyone overboard. For Hale, the shock of being tossed into the frigid water was followed by his disorientation in the dark water around him. He had plunged deep into the lake, and he had no immediate sense of the direction of the surface. He detected rising water bubbles and followed them to the surface. His muscles contracted in the forty-four-degree water, his peacoat, fully drenched, weighed him down. He frantically looked around. He could see no one. In the distance, thirty to forty feet away, a bright white light, the life raft's carbide light, designed to activate when the raft hit the water, cast a bright glow in the darkness. The raft was empty. Hale fought his way through the water, but swimming through the roiling seas was almost impossible, and he found that the raft would move away from him before he could reach it. Lake Huron's waves taunted him: the raft would disappear when it fell into a trough between waves, then it would be back in sight, still tantalizingly close as Hale tried to close the distance.

Hale pushed on, the bitter cold leaving him numb and his battle with the waves wearing him down. Time, as he would later note, had lost its definition. A long period seemed to have passed since he first heard the general alarm, but in reality it had been only a matter of minutes from the sound of the general alarm to his being tossed into the lake. He felt as if he had been in the water for an eternity, when, in fact, it had been a very

In this drawing, the forward crew of the *Daniel J. Morrell* gather on the life raft and await the inevitable. The torn stern section is in the background. Illustration by Robert McGreevy. Kenneth Thro Collection, University of Wisconsin–Superior.

brief amount of time. He was living in the moment, praying to survive until the next one.

His persistence eventually paid off. Two men—deckhands Art Stojek and John Cleary Jr.—had reached the raft before Hale, and they helped him climb aboard. Neither of the men was any more prepared than Hale to endure a lengthy stay on the raft. Stojek had slipped a life jacket over his pajamas. Cleary also wore a life jacket, but in jeans and a sweatshirt he was only slightly better prepared for what lay ahead of them. Both men, serving their first year on the lakes, appeared to be in shock. Cleary clung quietly to the raft, while Stojek worried about his chances of surviving in his thoroughly drenched pajamas. Both looked to Hale, the most experienced of the three, for leadership.

Hale edged his way to the raft's storage compartment, where parachute and handheld flares were stored. If there were any other vessels in the area, as Captain Crawley had suggested, they might be alerted by the parachute flares. It would have to happen soon. In this weather, the men would be suffering from hypothermia in no time. The three on the raft were in better shape than anyone in the water, but not by much. Hale's legs, exposed to the elements, were already numb.

Stojek and Cleary gathered at one side of the raft and called out to Hale. Someone was in the water nearby. By the time Hale had reached them, his two crewmates were pulling wheelsman Charles "Fuzzy" Fosbender from the lake. Fosbender had been on duty in the pilothouse when the Morrell began splitting in two, and despite his being soaked from his time in the lake, he was fully dressed and at least marginally more prepared than the others to face the climate. However, like the others, he seemed disoriented, perhaps in shock.

Opening the storage cabinet proved to be a difficult endeavor. The raft had been damaged when it was tossed overboard, and the door to the storage unit had been dented. The four men worked at it until they succeeded. Hale took out the flare gun and two of the six parachute flares in storage; the others reached in after him, each fumbling clumsily for anything useful. Hale fired two flares in the air. Neither rose as high as he hoped. Worse yet, the flare gun broke into two pieces when he fired it. He would have to hold the gun together if and when he attempted to fire more flares.

The men had only to look in the new distance to appreciate the severity of their plight. The Morrell's bow section, now a couple hundred yards away with the raft being blown away from it, was sinking steadily; only a small portion, pointed at the sky, remained afloat. Its silhouette was backlit by the still functioning lights on the stern. The stern, on the other hand, remained steady in the water and was now sailing away from the bow and the raft. It had nowhere to go but to the bottom of the lake, but it was impossible to predict how long it would take for water to flood through the gaping hole of the cargo hold and start the sinking process. In the meantime, the men onboard would have more time to consider how they might get off the boat and contemplate their best chances for survival. The lifeboats were out of the question: gale-force winds and heavy seas had made launching them unthinkable.

The men on the raft needed to find a way to stabilize their vessel. Although they were already drenched to their skin, with the howling wind making them even colder, they could not afford to have the waves hurling them overboard and back into the water. Hale searched in the storage compartment for the raft's sea anchor and oil can but could not find them.

The anchor would hold the raft in the water to some extent, while the oil can, when attached to the anchor, would periodically release oil to help calm the water close to the raft.

"Did anyone see the can of storm oil?" Hale shouted over the din of the storm. "Where is the sea anchor?"

Cleary had the sea anchor. Unfortunately, Stojek, thinking they had no use for the oil, had thrown the oil can overboard. Hale, naturally upset about Stojek's actions, was more concerned about his state of mind. Stojek was complaining in gibberish, and Hale worried about his succumbing to shock. They had to find a way to warm him, even if marginally, until help arrived.

Hale pulled out one of the handheld flares and lit it. The men grouped around it and held their hands near the flame. It did very little to help. Fosbender warned Hale about staying away from the liquid dripping off the flare, saying that it could burn a hole through his bare legs.

The storm, the growing distance between the raft and the two sections of the Morrell, the numbness overcoming the men's extremities, the confusion over where on Lake Huron they were actually located, the unlikelihood of their being rescued . . . all added to confusion that lacked immediate answers. In the darkness, the four men could barely make out the silhouette of the Morrell's bow as it slipped beneath the waves. Fosbender, seeing lights about a mile and a half away, grabbed the flashlight and tried to signal the potential rescue boat—until Hale told him that the lights, in fact, were from the stern section of the Morrell, still visible as it plowed through the storm.

The men, isolated on a bobbing raft on one of the largest freshwater bodies of water in the world, lost in a darkness so deep that it was unlikely that another vessel in the vicinity could find them, even if they saw a flare, settled in for what promised to be the longest night of their lives.

If, that is, they managed to survive it.

> > >

Other vessels shared the Morrell's and Townsend's struggles in the storm lashing Lake Huron. Most of the boats' captains wound up heading south along Michigan's eastern coastline until they reached sanctuary in Port Huron. When asked about their experiences, the captains agreed that the storm ranked high, if not at the top, of the worst storms they had ever encountered. The wind and high seas knocked them off course, pushed them into deadly troughs, even spun them around.

Captain Zernie Newman of the *Kinsman Independent*, a 592-footer carrying a load of coal, almost lost his boat in the eastern part of lower Michigan, near the Pointe Aux Barques Lighthouse, when he attempted to take shelter in Harbor Bay. Earlier that evening, at five thirty, winds had been light and out of the west, and the fifty-nine-year-old bulk carrier had little difficulty moving up Lake Huron. Assuming that the wind would shift to the northwest, Captain Newman took a course along Michigan's eastern coast, where the boat would be in the lee of the storm. Newman's assumption turned out to be incorrect. By the time the *Kinsman Independent* was sailing above Harbor Bay, the boat was facing heavy winds out of the north. Spun around by sixty-miles-per-hour winds at the height of the storm, the *Kinsman Independent* wound up trapped in a trough, caught between two huge waves. The boat's rudder failed to answer the pilothouse wheel, and the vessel faced the possibility of capsizing in the enormous waves crashing down on her. The boat eventually won the fight and sailed back down to Port Huron, but not before Newman took on what he estimated to be one of the worst storms of his career, second only to one on Lake Superior in 1952, when he had confronted twenty-five-foot waves built up by ninety-five-miles-per-hour winds.

Captain L. D. Jones had a similar experience when trying to guide his vessel, the *Howard L. Shaw*, through the building storm. There had been little sign of what lay ahead when the sixty-year-old, 451-foot freighter passed the Lake Huron Lightship at 3:45 p.m. on November 28, but like the *Kinsman Independent*, the *Shaw* found herself in the teeth of the storm when running abeam of Harbor Beach five and a half hours later. The boat could not hold its heading, and Jones's fight against nature became a struggle to keep his boat afloat, The *Shaw*, Jones would later tell the Coast Guard, was "spun around like a top." Jones made two attempts to push ahead before giving up and retreating to Port Huron.

One by one, powerful, reliable freighters surrendered to the forces of nature. The *Robert Hobson*, a 586-footer carrying coal, and the *Harry Coulby*, a 615-foot, thirty-nine-year-old bulk carrier, attempted to sail north, but both were stopped by weather, the *Coulby* when water washed over her deck and her skipper learned that he was heading into even worse conditions. The commander of the *Hobson*, Captain Charles D. Finch, later said that the speed of the wind did not surprise him, but that the height of the waves was greater than he had anticipated—"the worst continuously heavy seas I've ever been through."

The storm threatened vessels that were not sailing, as well. Two boats, grounded for days before the storm hit, stared at the prospects of being dismantled by waves and wind.

On the west side of Michigan, just inside the channel entrance to the Ludington harbor, a stranded boat awaited assistance. The *City of Midland 41*, a 407-foot car ferry, had been beached on a sandbar since November 27, the stormy weather too rough to permit either the disembarkment of passengers or assistance from a tugboat. The boat, carrying 128 passengers, 47 cars, several railroad freight cars, and a crew of 56, had left Manitowoc, Wisconsin, on one of the regularly scheduled runs to Ludington, a crossing of Lake Michigan that normally took a few hours. This trip, however, was different. The *Midland* sailed through a storm system that tossed the 4,000-ton ferry on waves built up by winds reaching eighty miles per hour. Blizzard snow reduced visibility, making Captain Henry Gates's entrance to the Ludington harbor a treacherous maneuver. The *Midland*, pushed by the wind, ran onto a sandbar and came to a sudden stop. Captain Gates ordered the ballast tanks filled. They were going nowhere until the bad weather subsided.

Fortunately for the passengers and crew, the *Midland* was well stocked with food and beverages, and she had nearly a two-week supply of fuel for heat and electricity. The *Midland* would take a beating from the waves, but it could have been worse: the harbor's breakwater would shield the *Midland* from the heaviest of the waves.

Two days passed. The bad weather intensified before showing signs of letting up. Representatives from the Chesapeake and Ohio Railway, owners of the *City of Midland*, assured the public that there was "absolutely no danger" to anyone onboard the car ferry; the passengers were warm and well fed. When the *Midland* ran short on meat, bread, milk, and eggs, the Coast Guard brought the provisions and passed them by rope to the disabled vessel.

On November 30, the day after the loss of the *Daniel J. Morrell*, while Hale clung to the life raft and the Coast Guard had begun the search for victims and survivors of the wreck, the *John Purves*, a 143-foot tug from Sturgeon Bay, Wisconsin, sailed across Lake Michigan and pulled into the Ludington Harbor, ready to assist in removing the *City of Midland* from the sandbar. The first attempts failed. Captain Gates had the water from

The bow of the tugboat *John Purvis* edges its way to the stranded *City of Midland* 41, preparing to tow the stricken passenger boat off a sandbar near Ludington, Michigan. Associated Press photograph; copyright AP Images.

the ballast tanks emptied. The tug finally freed the *Midland*, giving the Michigan news media an uplifting story to at least partially offset their sad duties of reporting the demise of the *Morrell*.

Another grounded vessel, not far from the *Morrell's* final location, was in much more desperate straits. The *Nordmeer*, a 470-foot German freighter hauling coiled steel, had run aground on November 19 on Thunder Bay Shoal, the impact tearing a long gash in the ship's bow. At first, no one was in immediate danger. The day after the beaching, crews began removing

The *City of Midland 41* was grounded on a sandbar on the Lake Michigan side of Michigan. After days of awaiting assistance in stormy weather, she was eventually towed to safety. No passengers were injured. Associated Press photograph by Alvan Quinn; copyright AP Images.

cargo from the *Nordmeer,* and all but Captain Ernst-George Steinbeck and seven of his crew were evacuated to safety. The eight remaining on the boat stayed there to prevent the twelve-year-old vessel from being claimed for salvage.

Now, however, there was a great sense of urgency: the *Nordmeer,* hammered by the storm, was in danger of being torn apart before the crew escaped. The boat had lost power, and the crew was in danger of freezing. At 3:03 a.m. on November 29, an hour after the loss of the *Morrell,* Captain Steinbeck transmitted an SOS, saying that the *Nordmeer* was taking water through the hatches. The *Nordmeer's* fore and aft cabins were filling with water, and the captain and crew, along with food and clothing, moved to the captain's cabin. The ship then lost her communications.

For hours, the Coast Guard was unable to provide any assistance. With no radio contact with the Coast Guard, the men on the *Nordmeer* feared the worst. The freighter slipped lower in the water. A desperate Captain Steinbeck fired flares into the air, hoping that there might be another boat in the area.

The Coast Guard cutter *Acacia* was directed to the area, but she was in trouble from the beginning, fighting seas and wind that held her progress

The *Nordmeer*, a 470-foot German freighter carrying coiled steel, ran aground on Thunder Bay Shoal on November 19. The storm started to pick her apart, and she began to sink. Only a dramatic rescue operation saved the crew members still onboard. Alpena News Collection, Alpena County George N. Fletcher Public Library.

An iced-over *Nordmeer* sunk to her spar deck and remained half-submerged until years later. Alpena News Collection, Alpena County George N. Fletcher Public Library.

Dennis Miller, in a photograph taken during the 1950s, installs a searchlight on the Coast Guard vessel *Acacia*. The 180-foot cutter assisted in the search and rescue operations for the *Morrell*. Courtesy of Dennis Miller.

to a minimum. Waves broke over her deck and tossed the vessel around like so much flotsam. Before being sent to the *Nordmeer*'s assistance, the *Acacia* had been sailing to Sault Ste. Marie, transporting two small Coast Guard craft—a 40-foot and a 36-foot boat—on her deck. The 36-footer broke loose in the heavy weather and banged around until it was held down by the *Acacia*'s boom.

"I've never been in a storm like it," Dennis Miller, an electrician aboard the *Acacia*, recalled. "Never before, never since." The lake had been calm when the *Acacia* headed out in the afternoon, but by evening, when the *Acacia* was directed to assist the *Nordmeer*, the wind had shifted from the north, and the Coast Guard cutter was rolling so badly that Miller found it difficult to maintain his balance while he was walking. For the first time in his sailing on the lakes, he was sick. The cyclometer in the wheelhouse, he remembered, showed the boat rolling at thirty degrees. A Pepsi machine broke free and slid about the floor.

"We took a wave down the stack that flooded the engine room," he continued. "The first class engineman called the captain and said, 'We have to turn around and get back to Port Huron or we're lost.'"

Fearing for the safety of his crew and vessel, Charles Millradt, the *Acacia*'s commander, heeded the engineer's advice. "We were bouncing around like you wouldn't believe," he remembered. Harbor Beach, his first choice of shelter, was now impossible in the raging seas. "We couldn't line up with the breakwater," Millradt explained. He wound up making a run for Port Huron. The *Acacia* took a beating all the way down the eastern coast of Michigan, but she arrived safely and tied up, the men onboard hoping to wait out the storm.

The Coast Guard was running out of options on rescuing the crew on the *Nordmeer*. The *Mackinaw* was nearby, but monstrous waves kept the *Mackinaw* or any other potential rescue vessel from drawing close to the *Nordmeer*. Helicopters were similarly hindered by gale-force winds. Heavy snow fell, and visibility dropped. A rescue mission was simply out of the question.

Conditions had improved, but not by much, the next morning. The wind velocity was down, but Lake Huron's waves were still very rough, and it was still snowing. With time running out for the *Nordmeer*, the Coast Guard decided to attempt a helicopter rescue.

In Detroit, the Coast Guard Air Station dispatched a helicopter to assist in the *Nordmeer* rescue. The 150-mile flight from Detroit Air Station to the M/V *Nordmeer* was conducted under weather conditions that "severely tested the skill and courage of the crew," J. W. Swanson, the commandant of the Detroit station, wrote later. "From shortly after take-off, low ceilings and icing conditions forced the aircraft to fly only 300 feet above the terrain in snow showers with visibility reduced to one half mile at times. The final eighty miles of the route [were] flown in nearly continuous snow and light icing conditions at 200 feet over Lake Huron utilizing the shine for navigation. After two hours and thirty-four minutes of demanding, low level flight and still encountering adverse weather conditions the helicopter located the M/V *Nordmeer*."

Then the storm unexpectedly let up. The Coast Guard helicopter moved in and pulled all eight sailors from the *Nordmeer*'s deck and deposited them on the *Mackinaw*, stationed nearby. The men were lifted by bucket, one at a time, to the helicopter, which had to hover in wind gusts still high enough to make the procedure very risky. Lowering the men to the *Mackinaw*'s icy deck was also hazardous. "Luckily, no one was hurt," said Lonnie Mixon, who copiloted the helicopter and received the Distinguished Flying Cross for his efforts.

The storied Coast Guard icebreaker *Mackinaw* assisted in the search for the *Daniel J. Morrell's* lost crew members. She also headed the rescue operations for the *Nordmeer*. U.S. Coast Guard photograph.

It was also fortunate that the rescuers worked as quickly as they did. Picking up the German sailors took twenty-two minutes. By the time the last man was removed, the *Nordmeer's* deck was awash. Only minutes later, the vessel began to split apart and sank farther in the water.

"God was real nice to us," said Jack Rittichier, the helicopter's other copilot, awarded the Coast Guard's Air Medal for his actions in the rescue mission. "The storm broke as we moved in. All of a sudden things cleared up. As soon as the last man was picked up, it began to snow again."

Mixon agreed that good timing and fortune helped them avert a tragedy. They had considered and rejected the idea of stopping and deicing the helicopter before heading out over the water in search of the *Nordmeer*. When they initially had no luck in locating the boat, they thought about heading back to land, but they decided to continue the search for a couple more minutes. In that short period of time, they found the German freighter. Finally, they wondered if it might be best to take the first four recovered seamen to Wurthsmith before returning to the *Nordmeer* for the remaining four; they wound up taking them to the *Mackinaw* instead.

"Had we gone to Wurthsmith, we wouldn't have gotten back to the *Nordmeer* in time," Mixon stated. "Or, had we not stayed out those two extra minutes, we wouldn't have found the *Nordmeer* in time to get everyone off."

The wreck, in water so shallow that her masts remained above water after the sinking, would eventually become a popular diving site. Her German owner never attempted to salvage her.

> > >

"What do you think our chances are?" Cleary asked Hale.

"A lot better than the guys who didn't make it to the raft with us," Hale replied.

Cleary, frightened by the odds against his survival, was soaking wet and very cold. The twenty-year-old deckhand had been on the raft only for a short time before he started showing signs of the onset of hypothermia. He sounded drowsy to Hale, and he was slurring his words. Hale urged him to stay awake.

At twenty, Cleary was the second-youngest crew member onboard the *Morrell*. He was bright, creative, and very good at working with his hands. As a boy, he had built model railroads with his father, complete with surrounding balsa wood cities, in the basement of their Cleveland home. When he grew into his teens, Cleary enjoyed working on cars. He and his father grew distant during his later teen years, and Cleary had signed up for work on the boats as a way of avoiding further bickering with his father.

Charles "Fuzzy" Fosbender, one of the four men to board the *Morrell*'s life raft after the boat's sinking. Badly injured during the sinking, Fosbender survived the stormy night on Lake Michigan but perished the next day. Courtesy of Mary Lou Harrington Szmytkowski.

Of the three other men on the raft, Hale probably identified with Cleary the most. He was closest to Cleary in age, and he could certainly empathize with Cleary's problems with his father. Fosbender and Stojek lived far more settled, sedate lives. Both worried about how their wives would fare if they failed to make it off the raft alive. Cecilia Stojek was especially vulnerable. Art supported her, their four children, and her parents, who lived with them. He had been laid off from his upstate New York job about two months earlier and took a job on the boats as a last resort.

Now, unless circumstances changed dramatically, these would be the last men Hale would see in his life.

Weather conditions looked ominous as the *Bramble* headed out on her last day searching for the wreckage of the *Daniel J. Morrell*. Photograph by Roland Schultz, QM-1 U.S. Coast Guard.

GAUNTLETS OF HOPE
AND DESPAIR

THE WAVES, RELENTLESS AND PITILESS, WEAKENED THE MEN'S resolve. The first had hit them not long after they climbed onto the life raft. Dennis Hale had seen it before the others. It advanced toward the raft, a black mass twenty-five to thirty feet in height. Hale lay on his side on the wooden slats of the raft, clutched a steel rod running from side to side on the raft, and braced himself against the wall of water he expected to come crashing down on him. The wave, however, did not crash down; the raft *passed through* it. The force of the rushing water was nearly enough to tear the men from the raft, but they managed to hold on. Hale held his breath, wondering how long he would be buried in the icy water.

The wave passed. The four men, thoroughly drenched and gasping for air, now faced another type of torture: they had to deal with the gale-force wind that ripped through their saturated clothing. It burned, and there was no immediate relief. Hale felt as if something was peeling his skin away.

The burning sensation, he would write in his autobiography, lasted for only a brief period of time. After that, his body went numb—until the next giant wave assaulted them. The first extinguished the raft's carbide lights. In the darkness, the men couldn't see the next approaching wave; they were constantly on edge, awaiting the worst. When they first climbed aboard the raft, they had huddled together and talked as a form of mutual encouragement. They discussed their changes of being rescued, the odds of their being discovered before morning, and what they would do when they were warm again. They fell silent as time passed.

Hale's mood swung from supplication in prayer to a desire to die and have his suffering come to an end. His bare legs had lost all feeling. He tried to help his circulation and generate warmth by stretching and moving his legs and ankles; he put his hands in his mouth to keep them from cramping or freezing. He urged his crewmates to stay awake.

In the early hours of the morning, before daybreak, the storm began to subside. It quit snowing. More and more time passed between the monster waves, and then they ceased altogether. The men continued to absorb a terrible punishment from the wind. The day broke cloudy and gray, with another threat of rain or snow.

The men lay motionless in the positions they had held throughout the night. Hale lay on his left side in the middle of the raft, with John Cleary, facedown on his stomach, to Hale's right. Art Stojek curled into a fetal position to Hale's left, and Fuzzy Fosbender positioned himself below him. Hale could make out Cleary's facial features in the dawn light, and he appeared to be in very bad condition. He was pale, and a white foam came from his mouth.

Hale poked at him but received no response.

"John, are you all right?" Hale asked. "John, wake up, man. Are you okay?" Hale repeatedly jabbed at the young deckhand, to no avail. He did not move, and he did not answer Hale's calls. He had passed away during the night.

When he tried to rouse Stojek, Hale discovered that he, too, had died. Hale panicked, gripped by a fear that he might be the only one alive on the raft. He was terrified by the prospects of being alone.

To his great relief, Fosbender responded when he called out to him. Fosbender told Hale that he was OK, that he had spent the night praying. The two tried to stay optimistic about their chances of being discovered and rescued. It all depended on how soon somebody on land realized the *Morrell* was missing, or when a vessel happened across wreckage or the bodies of lost crewmen. Hale speculated that they would be picked up sometime during the afternoon.

This was how it had gone with the *Carl D. Bradley* eight years earlier. The *Bradley* had broken in two in the late-afternoon hours, just as it was getting dark, and the two survivors of the wreck had ridden out the night and early hours of the next day on a raft similar to the one now occupied by the four men from the *Morrell*. Unlike the *Morrell*, the *Bradley* had transmitted an

SOS. Ports all around the lakes knew that the *Bradley* had sunk. A German freighter had seen a column of fire erupt from the *Bradley's* smokestack when the stern sank and cold water hit her boilers, causing an immense explosion. The freighter sailed immediately in the direction of the fire, but between the pitch black of the evening and the enormous waves more than capable of hiding a life raft in the troughs between the waves, there was no hope of finding survivors until the following day. The raft was found in the middle of the next morning.

Both men on the *Morrell's* life raft realized that time was working against Fosbender. Although he did not complain about his condition, Fosbender had been seriously injured when he was thrown off the bow section of the sinking *Morrell*. His chest and shoulders were crushed, and there was no telling what kind of internal injuries he might have sustained. He desperately needed medical attention. By the afternoon hours of November 29, twelve hours after the breaking up of the *Morrell*, Fosbender was barely hanging on, the combination of his injuries and the bitter cold stealing what little life he had left. He developed a painful, hacking cough.

The two survivors kept their thoughts to themselves. Hale spent much of his time thinking about his fellow crewmates on the *Morrell*, especially the two lost on the raft. He scanned the horizon for any sign of people searching for them—a Coast Guard cutter, a helicopter, anything. He doubted that anyone knew that the *Morrell* was missing. He let his mind roam. He fantasized that he was in a lush green, tropical setting, his body tanned and warm. He prayed for help, or if he wasn't going to get divine intervention, that he would die soon.

"I can see land."

Fosbender's voice brought Hale back to the cold present.

"How close are we, Fuzz?"

"We're not even close." Land, Fosbender said, was distant, but the raft was drifting in its direction.

Hale, positioned on his side in a way that found him looking in the opposite direction, didn't even attempt to look for himself.

"We had oars," he would remember, "but we didn't have the strength to row. We were frozen and cold." They would have been in similarly bad shape even if they had reached land. In the event that the raft was beached onshore, both men were too weak to walk any great distance. They would still have to be discovered.

They allowed themselves hope. They talked about how good it would be to be home for the holidays, how their wives wouldn't believe it when they heard about the *Morrell* and their surviving it.

Something had to happen soon. Fosbender told Hale that it was about two o'clock, which meant they had only about two and a half hours of daylight left. Another night on the lake, in subfreezing temperatures, was unthinkable.

Fosbender's cough grew worse as the afternoon progressed and dusk grew near. Land, he told Hale, was close enough that he could see the rocks and boulders in the shallow water near the shoreline. It wouldn't be long before their raft was grounded.

"Maybe someone will see us," Hale offered.

"Well, they better hurry," Fosbender replied feebly, "because it feels like my lungs are filling up."

Hale suggested that Fosbender try to hack out some of whatever was clogging his lungs. He tried, but it didn't work. He had pulled himself up for a better look toward the shore, bracing himself with one hand on the deck of the raft and the other on Hale's leg.

"I'm going to throw in the sponge," he told Hale.

He made one final attempt to cough, then collapsed lifeless into Hale.

Hale was overwhelmed by a feeling of defeat. His fear of being left alone on the raft had come to pass. How could he expect to survive when he was surrounded by three friends who had been brought down by hypothermia? He was tired, hungry, thirsty, frostbitten, and unbearably cold, dying from exposure. Cold water still washed over the side of the raft, though the wind and waves were nowhere near as imposing as they had been the previous evening.

The raft finally grounded on rocks jutting out of the water. The raft, pushed by the wind, swung around, giving Hale a clear view at the shore, which he estimated to be about two hundred yards away. He saw rocks, trees, and, a short distance inland, what appeared to be a farmhouse. Lights shone from within the structure.

The raft had come to rest in very shallow water. Less than twenty-four hours ago, Hale could have easily made his way to shore; he was now too weak to climb off the raft, let alone walk to safety.

He shouted for help, and when he received no answer, he fired his last remaining flare.

Still no response. He had no choice but to steel himself for the worst:

he had more than twelve hours of darkness ahead of him, and if the weather conditions weren't imposing enough already, it began to snow again.

> > >

A second night in the open air: Hale dozed briefly from time to time, only to awaken to the dark reality. The lights in the distant house were off, clouds blocked the moon and stars. Hale concentrated on what he felt he needed to do to survive. He had fought to stay awake out of fear that he might die if he fell asleep. He had even refrained from urinating out of a fear of losing internal heat. The lack of food, the shivering, and other bodily efforts to generate heat had carved nearly twenty-five pounds from his husky frame. He prayed for relief.

Life or death: Hale was conflicted. His suffering and depression were so immense that, at one point, he decided to end his life. "Death," he would admit later, was "the window to my mind."

He considered removing his peacoat, shorts, and life jacket, which would undoubtedly lead to his freezing to death, but he was too weak to do so. He then came up with the idea of jamming his fingers down his throat and suffocating. This only led to a lot of coughing and gagging. This wore him out, even though it did generate a little warmth. He gave up and fell asleep.

Toward daybreak, Hale saw the lights blink back on in the house. He shouted for help, but with his strength almost gone, he was unable to shout loud enough or sustain the shouting for any length of time. The only positive to come out of the effort was it made him feel slightly warmer.

He looked over at Cleary. Ice had formed on his hands and clothing. The thought of seeing this young man encased in ice, his life ended when he should have had so many years ahead of him, infuriated Hale. The other two had reached middle age. Losing them had been hard enough, but Cleary hadn't lived half as long. Early on, not long after they had gathered on the raft, Cleary, called "Butch" by his fellow crewmen, asked Hale to look up his girlfriend in the event that he didn't make it out alive, to "let her know he loved her."

Hale pulled himself up on one elbow and shook a fist at the sky. He cursed his God for all that was happening, for making him suffer. Then, in what he would later describe as "an act of love, compassion, and envy," he reached over and picked the ice off Cleary's hands.

"I was filled with empathy for this young boy," he would remember. "I started picking the ice off his hands. It was the final insult. I cursed at God."

He drifted off to sleep a short time later.

❯ ❯ ❯

Hale's confinement to the raft gave him ample opportunity to ponder the events of his life. Shortly after all four men had climbed onboard the raft, Cleary had asked Hale about his family, and Hale told him about his wife, Bertha, and their two children and his two stepchildren. The conversations had been brief, but after the passing of his three crewmates, Hale thought about what his life had delivered him thus far.

It had never been easy. His mother, Ruby Hale, had died shortly after giving birth to him on January 23, 1940, in their Cleveland home; she had been rushed to the hospital, but she had hemorrhaged so badly after giving birth to an eleven-pound baby that she could not be saved. All Dennis knew of her was what he saw in photographs or from the sketchy details provided by others. "The events of that night tore my family apart and destroyed any chance I might have had of having a normal childhood," he wrote in *Sole Survivor*, the first of his two book-length accounts of his life.

Clayter Hale, Dennis's father, owned an auto repair garage, and he had been unable to raise his four children—Dennis had two older brothers, Robert and Edward, and a sister, Jean—so he shipped them off to relatives. From then on, Dennis rarely saw or heard from his father or brothers. He tried to keep open a small line of communication with his sister, with only marginal success.

It might be said that Hale spent his childhood and youth in search of a family. He was taken in by his Aunt Inez and Uncle Vern Harrison, who had five children of their own, all much older than Hale. Their son, Harold, was overseas, serving in the navy during World War II. The four daughters lived at home. They looked after Hale, who regarded them as family; he called his aunt "Mom." This ended when Hale was about four, when his aunt called him in from outside and explained that she was not his mother, despite the way she treated him.

Hale's life changed dramatically when Harold returned home at the end of the war. Harold disliked Dennis, and whenever they were out of eyesight and earshot of Inez, Harold berated his cousin, telling him that he had killed his mother and was worthless; just as damaging, he physically and, later, sexually abused him. Hale, who had idolized Harold when he returned home from the service, tried to survive the mistreatment by avoiding him whenever possible. In time, the Harrison girls married and moved away. Harold became even more ruthless after his parents split up and divorced, and Inez moved Harold and Dennis to Los Angeles. Hale felt that his aunt either could not or would not address the issue with her son. Day-to-day life could be a scene from Dickens.

Hale's life took another downward turn during his teenage years. He fell in with some of the tougher kids in his school—when he even bothered to go to school—and he got into minor trouble with the law when he and others stole cars for joyriding. He ran away from home when Inez attempted to return him to his father, who had remarried and was living on a farm in Ashtabula. He wound up spending two years with his father and his new family, but it was far from an ideal environment. His father barely knew him, and Hale felt that he was little more than someone kept around to do chores around the farmyard and house. By his own admission, his self-esteem plummeted.

"My father and I had no relationship," Hale would recall. "He very seldom even talked to me. He wasn't mean or abrupt. He just didn't seem to have anything to say to me. It was as though he wanted no relationship with me at all."

When he reached the end of his patience for living with his father, Hale did what by now had become all too familiar: he ran. He would hitchhike, or when he grew a little older and saved money from different jobs, he would catch a bus for the West Coast. His life became a cycle of questionable decisions. He would make his way back to Los Angeles, his father would learn where he was staying, and he would be shipped back to Ohio, where he would stay until he ran away the next time. As a minor, he was bound to be returned to his father, and since he was usually turned in to his father by a relative he was staying with, Hale distrusted everyone.

He eventually found himself back in Los Angeles for an extended period of time. He found a room and a job, and returned to high school. He kept his plans and living arrangements to himself. He avoided his old set of friends. Between work and high school, he had little time for trouble.

But he needed a sense of family, even one as dysfunctional as his own; he needed to *belong*. After his graduation from high school, he returned to Ashtabula and took a room in the YMCA. His father, he reasoned, wouldn't be willing to take him back. He was correct in this thinking. When he and his father finally met, the reception was lukewarm. There was no discussion about Hale's moving back in with the family.

Sometime earlier, while living on his father's farm in Ohio, Hale began attending church services. His father had little interest in religious matters, but his father's wife, Chick, was religious. She patiently answered Hale's questions about her faith and practices. Hale found Catholicism comforting, something that gave meaning to his life.

"I knew that becoming Catholic would fill a void in my heart," he wrote, "and only then would I feel like I really belonged."

That had been in an earlier life with his father. After graduating from high school and returning to Ashtabula, he felt he had to move on. He enlisted in the army, but it went poorly. He was shipped off to France, where he met a woman in Paris, stayed with her for three days without alerting his superiors of his absence, and was considered AWOL. He was court-martialed and given a thirty-day sentence, although when he left the army, he was given an honorable discharge.

Hale liked to cook, and he worked several jobs in the kitchen after he returned to the United States. At one of the jobs, at the Hotel Ashtabula, he met his future wife, Bertha, who was also employed at the hotel's restaurant. She was seven years his senior, divorced, and had two children. When he married Bertha, Dennis found himself immersed in a new family. Their marriage was full of ups and downs, especially after they added two children of their own and Hale found that he had to scramble to support his growing family. When he learned that he could earn substantially more money by working on the big ore carriers, he looked into it, despite his healthy fear of storms.

The *Daniel J. Morrell* was his first boat. He hooked up with the vessel in 1964 and never looked back. Life on the Great Lakes felt like home.

❯ ❯ ❯

At noon on November 30, unbeknownst to Hale, Bethlehem Steel called the Coast Guard Rescue Coordination Center in Cleveland and reported the *Daniel J. Morrell* as missing. Thirty-four hours had passed since the boat had broken apart.

Concern over the *Morrell*'s whereabouts had begun the previous day, when the *Morrell* was required to radio a position report to Bethlehem

The *Edward Y. Townsend*, once one of the sturdiest vessels on the Great Lakes, never sailed after the storm that claimed the *Daniel J. Morrell*. Kenneth Thro Collection, University of Wisconsin–Superior.

Steel's office in Cleveland. Art Dobson, the chief dispatcher at the office, had heard from the *Townsend*. The *Morrell's* failure to report, while troublesome, did not raise too much concern. The *Morrell* had not reported any problems in previous communications. There had been no SOS or other indications of trouble. The *Townsend*, sailing in similar conditions, had come through all right. It was possible that the storm had disabled the *Morrell's* radio antenna, that she had ducked out of the storm somewhere and had been unable to report it. Freighters were known to "go missing" in storms—over the years, some had been reported as lost with all hands—only to turn up later, when waters had calmed enough to enable them to sail again.

At two in the afternoon, five hours after the time the *Morrell* was scheduled to contact him, Dobson spoke again to Captain Thomas Connelly.

The *Townsend* was still on Lake Huron, headed to the Soo Locks. Connelly was growing concerned about the *Morrell*. The last time he had spoken to Captain Crawley, Connelly told Dobson, had been 12:15 a.m. that morning. He had tried to contact the *Morrell* an hour and a half later, at 1:45, and again at 3:45, but he received nothing but dead air. The *Morrell* had been sailing about fifteen to twenty miles ahead of the *Townsend*. Somebody should have seen or heard from the boat by now.

Dobson asked Connelly to continue in his efforts to contact the *Morrell*; he then contacted the *Arthur B. Homer*, another Bethlehem Steel ore carrier, and asked that the crew be on the lookout for the missing boat. Dobson himself made numerous attempts to contact the *Morrell*. By nightfall—and the beginning of Hale's second night on the lake—with still no contact, Dobson began to suspect the worst.

There was more troubling news the following morning. The *Townsend* had reached the St. Marys River and the Lime Island fueling station, and while refueling, Captain Connelly had discovered a crack on his boat's spar deck. He radioed Dobson with the news, saying that the *Townsend* would be docked until further notice. Dobson, who had not heard from the *Morrell* for yet another scheduled reporting time, knew that something serious had happened. If the *Morrell* had been sailing twenty miles ahead of the *Townsend*, she should have been seen or heard from on the St. Marys River. Despite the repeated efforts by Dobson, Bethlehem Steel, and the masters of several boats on Lake Huron, no one had been able to contact the *Morrell*.

At 12:15, Bethlehem Steel called the Rescue Coordination Center and formally reported the *Daniel J. Morrell* as missing. The Coast Guard responded immediately, assembling an all-out search and rescue effort. Not that there was much hope for a rescue: if the *Morrell* had gone down between 12:15 a.m., when Connelly had last spoken to Crawley, and 1:45 a.m., when Connelly unsuccessfully tried to call the boat on the morning of November 29, it was very unlikely that anyone would be found alive—not after nearly a day and a half in conditions that would have killed a man in the water in, at best, an hour or two.

While the Cleveland Coast Guard scurried to assemble a team of freighters, Coast Guard cutters, fixed-wing aircraft, and helicopters to search for the *Morrell*, a crewman on the *C. G. Post*, a freighter sailing about eight miles north of the Harbor Beach Breakwater Lighthouse, saw a body floating face down in the water.

The man wore an orange life jacket with *Daniel J. Morrell* stenciled on it.

Huron City Coast Guard Station

The Huron City Coast Guard station, located near the top of lower Michigan's "thumb," was active in the search for the *Morrell*'s crew. Courtesy of the Detroit Historical Society.

❯ ❯ ❯

Hale spent that same morning of November 30 hoping that someone would see the bright-red pontoon raft that had become his prison. He was now in the throes of an advancing stage of hypothermia, drifting in and out of consciousness, sometimes sleeping, occasionally hallucinating, never quite certain if what he was seeing was real or imagined. At times, he thought he heard helicopters or airplanes overhead, but the sounds turned out to be seagulls.

He had his first visionary experience shortly after awakening from another brief period of sleep. He was terribly thirsty, and in an irony that could only be appreciated by someone who had spent a day and a half on a body of fresh water, he could find no way to get a drink. For a good portion of his time on the raft, he had used a piece of the broken flare gun as a cup, filling it with lake water and judiciously parceling out just enough to slake his thirst without compromising his body temperature. At some point, he had lost the gun.

He pulled himself up on his left elbow and looked around. He could not locate the gun or anything else that he might use to hold water. He did find another possibility: he was covered in ice and snow. He pulled some of the ice from his peacoat's collar and ate it, letting it all melt in his mouth and roll down his throat. He had barely begun when, as he would recall, "it really [got] quiet, very quiet."

He felt as if he was being watched. He looked up and saw a man with white, wavy hair standing at the edge of the raft. The man had bushy eyebrows, a white beard, and a neatly trimmed mustache. His skin was very pale, almost translucent, with a hint of a bluish tint. He wore a robe.

"Stop eating the ice off your coat," he commanded. He then disappeared as suddenly as he had appeared.

Hale did as instructed. He dropped back to the raft and thought about "Doc," as he nicknamed the apparition. Had the old man actually spoken to him, or was it something he simply heard in his mind? For the brief time he had stood at the edge of the raft, Hale judged him to be very intense yet kind. His voice had been "thunderous."

Hale had little time to mentally process the old man's visitation. Within minutes of his disappearance, Hale had another experience he would be hard-pressed to explain. In this hallucination, he began to rise off the raft until he was floating in the air, amid the clouds, looking down on the raft. Hale wondered if he had died and was now looking at his former reality moments after his passing. But his ascent was not yet complete. He kept rising, eventually at a very high rate of speed. He was not frightened. He felt as if he was being transported to a place that was calm and loving.

He arrived in a land he had never seen before, with a landscape of bright, vivid colors. In the distance, a bridge crossed over a valley, and on the other side of the bridge stood Hale's mother and other dead relatives. However, before he could cross the bridge, he had to secure the permission of a handful of white-clad men and women—people dressed very similar to "Doc." Their leader, a heavyset, balding man who reminded

Hale of Friar Tuck, motioned him over and, taking his hands, said, "Let us see what you've learned." As Hale and the man watched, scenes from Hale's life were projected onto Hale's hands. Hale was happy with some of what he saw, but some of the scenes made him cringe. The man assured him that it was all right, that he had learned from the experiences. When the brief biography ended, the man allowed Hale to cross the bridge.

The reunion with his relatives was awkward. He embraced his mother and was overjoyed to see her, but since she had died at his birth, he didn't know her well enough to say much to her. He didn't know some of the others, relatives who had passed away before he was born.

Hale asked about his shipmates and learned they were at the bottom of a hill. Hale told his family members that he needed to see them and excused himself.

The bow portion of the *Morrell*, as it had been after breaking away from the storm, stood at the bottom of the hill. Hale scaled a ladder to board the boat. His shipmates from the forward section of the *Morrell* were all there.

"They gathered around me and hugged me, and told me how glad they were to see me," Hale wrote in *Sole Survivor*. "Their behavior was not typical of Great Lakes sailors, since everyone I met there were seemed very innocent and childlike."

No one mentioned the wreck. While they gathered, the stern portion of the *Morrell* approached from a distance and rejoined the bow section where they had separated.

Hale and the others headed to the engine room in the back of the boat, where they joined the rest of the *Morrell*'s crew. Everyone, Hale would remember, was "yelling and laughing and hugging each other."

"The time I was in the cloud all you could feel was love around you," he told Steve Kuchera of the *Duluth News Tribune* in 2012. "It was the same way when I was greeted by my shipmates. It was a beautiful thing."

Unfortunately for Hale, the reunion was short-lived. George Dahl, the *Morrell*'s third engineer, put an end to the merriment.

"Dennis, what are you doing here?" he asked. "It's not your time yet. You have to go back."

And with that, Hale was whisked back to the raft and the reality of the endless cold, pain, and suffering—everything as it was before his vision of heaven. He again picked at the ice on his collar, and once again, the old man appeared and, with a shake of his left index finger, extended his warning.

"I told you not to eat the ice off your peacoat," he said. "If you do, you'll lower your body temperature and die."

Hale quit eating the ice. He resolved to heed Doc's advice from this point forward.

> > >

Hale listened with disinterest to the sound of seagulls flying overhead. Seagulls had been flying around the area, off and on, all day. Hale paid them little attention, other than to wonder why they didn't alert someone of his presence near the shore. Night would be falling in the next hour or so. His coat and legs were now covered with ice; he no longer had a trace of feeling in his feet. He struggled to distinguish between reality and illusion. He understood that few people would believe him when he spoke of all he had seen over the past few hours, but the visions seemed realistic and detailed enough to be more than dreams or hallucinations. Between his physical and mental conditions, he wondered if he could survive a third night on the water. He doubted it.

"I figured maybe through the next night that I would freeze—it was really cold," he would remember. "It iced all over the boat. . . . I was hoping to die. I was in terrible pain."

Hale propped himself on an elbow. Something about the noise overhead was different from the seagull sounds he had heard throughout the day. It was louder than a flock of seagulls, and it sounded like helicopter blades. Of course, he had thought this before, only to look up and see winged scavengers flying overhead.

However, this time he was not hearing birds. A helicopter hovered over the raft. Hale summoned the energy to wave feebly at it. The helicopter had pontoons; it landed on the water near the raft. Two men sloshed through knee-deep water toward the raft while a second helicopter touched down on the other side of the raft.

Hale was too weak to move.

"I love ya," he said when his rescuers arrived at the raft. "I love ya . . . I love ya . . . I love ya."

> > >

Dennis Hale's thirty-eight-hour ordeal came to an end when his raft was spotted by a Coast Guard helicopter. He was carefully removed from the raft and raced to Harbor Beach. Photograph by Ralph Polovich, Port Huron *Times Herald*.

Hale proved to be too difficult for two men to move, so Al Massey, a coastguardsman from the helicopter on the other side of the raft, waded across the water to assist.

Recovering the other three men on the raft was difficult, gruesome work. The sailors were encased in ice; icicles dangled from their ears and noses. "The bodies were frozen like statues," Massey recalled, "in the positions they were in when they died."

The coastguardsmen labored to remove the bodies from the raft, walk each of the dead crewmen across the water to the awaiting helicopter, and, perhaps most difficult of all, fit them through the door and into the limited space in the helicopter's cabin. The three crewmen were then flown to Harbor Beach.

The discovery of a survivor lifted the spirits of those in the search and rescue mission. After all the tedious searching and depressing results of finding only victims floating on the water, the men in the Coast Guard were elated to learn that the work had produced positive results.

A massive search began as soon as the loss of the *Morrell* became evident. Coast Guard stations from all over Michigan contributed helicopters, planes, and boats, and citizen volunteers walked the coastlines in search of victims. Photograph by Ralph Polovich, Port Huron *Times Herald*.

"There was a lot of hootin' and hollerin' on the *Mackinaw* when they announced that they'd found a survivor," recalled Art Lind, who was a yeoman onboard the *Mackinaw* when Hale was picked up from the raft.

An ambulance met the helicopter carrying Hale. The helicopter landed in a Harbor Beach parking lot near the city's marina, and Hale was carefully carried to the ambulance. The helicopter ride from the raft to land had taken all of five minutes, by Hale's estimation. On the way, he saw a thermos of coffee on the helicopter, but his rescuers told him they were under strict orders not to give him anything to eat or drink.

"We told the man to rest and that we wouldn't try to ask questions right away about the sinking," said Lt. Commander Benjamin S. Beach, the helicopter pilot transporting Hale to the hospital, "but he said, 'No, no, that's all right, I want someone to talk to me.'" After so much time in solitude, Hale was ready for any kind of conversation.

"Hale had no trousers or shoes on, yet his bulk and the protection given by his shipmates' bodies appeared to have made his survival possible," noted Lt. William H. Hall, another coastguardsman on the scene. Hall's observation would be echoed by hospital personal attending Hale. It would even be suggested that his lack of trousers might have helped save his life: if he had been wearing pants, they would have been soaked and frozen, further lowering his body temperature.

Those at the hospital made the same observations as the coast-guardsmen: Hale was in remarkably good condition, given all he had been through. Other than a cut on his neck and some skin missing from abrasions on two fingers, he had suffered no significant injuries from being thrown off the boat and spending so much time on the raft. His legs were blue, with purple blotches, and his feet were frostbitten and blistered. His body temperature registered 94.6 degrees.

Burton E. Ramsey, owner of a funeral home and one of those assisting with Hale's transportation to the hospital, told reporters that he saw a man who had nearly frozen to death. "When I lifted his head, I could feel the ice on his neck," he said.

"It was the coldest I ever felt anybody that was alive," said Dr. Robert Oakes, the first to see Hale at the hospital. Hale, he recalled, was covered with ice when he was admitted.

Oakes was a contract doctor for the Coast Guard, as had been his father, Dr. Charles W. Oakes. When he was told that the Coast Guard had picked up a half-frozen man on a raft, Oakes expected the worst. What he found was a man suffering from hypothermia, frostbite, and dehydration, but reasonably lucid, all things considered. Hale was able to answer questions about his medical history and what he had experienced on the raft.

The twenty-eight-bed hospital had never worked on a patient in this condition, so Oakes consulted the Henry Ford Hospital in Detroit about treatment options for Hale. Blood clots, he was told, could be a major concern, and one had to monitor the rise in body temperature, taking caution about how quickly it rose. After stitching Hale's neck, Oakes and other hospital staff wrapped Hale's legs and feet in bandages. He was offered some warm consommé, but he couldn't drink it

Father Cornelius McEachin, a Roman Catholic priest, visited, heard a sacramental confession, and read Hale his last rites. Receiving the last rights came unexpectedly to Hale: he had assumed that he was safe now that the raft had been discovered and he had been delivered to doctors and nurses.

"I had thought that death was behind me now," he wrote in his memoir *Shipwrecked*. "I figured that now that they had found me I was safe and death was not even an option."

Word of Hale's survival spread quickly, and the press rushed to the hospital, hoping to obtain details about the *Morrell*'s sinking and Hale's survival. Hale had yet to speak to his wife, and with the Coast Guard was still searching for other survivors, Hale did not want to speak to the press. Ruth Wintenhalter, director of the hospital, kept reporters at bay. As an added precaution, Hale's bed was eventually wheeled into the hospital's maternity ward.

Even if Hale had been physically capable of meeting the press, he was probably too fragile, emotionally and mentally, to talk about his ordeal. He continually thought about the three men who had been with him on the raft, and obsessed about his other shipmates. Had any of them been picked up? If he had survived, maybe others had survived as well. With two lifeboats and a life raft stored on the stern of the *Morrell*, wasn't it possible that one or more had been launched? He couldn't bear the thought of being the shipwreck's only survivor.

What he did not know—and would not know until the following day, when he saw several newspapers—was just how many of the *Morrell*'s crew were being pulled from the lake.

> > >

Finding Hale alive had been a miracle, and while the Coast Guard did not expect to find others—too long a time had passed, the weather conditions too extreme for survival—the Dennis Hale story led to the faintest of hopes.

The discovery of the first body of a *Morrell* crewman also pushed the Coast Guard's search and rescue mission to a new level of urgency. Commercial freighters were asked to stay alert for bodies and wreckage in the water. Coast Guard stations from all around Michigan joined the search. Harbor Beach sent two small boats to look for victims or survivors; stations in Port Huron and Saginaw River sent boats. Two helicopters from Detroit flew up, while Traverse City kicked in two helicopters and two fixed-wing aircraft. Three large Coast Guard vessels—the *Acacia*, *Bramble*, and *Mackinaw*—rushed to the area. The U.S. Coast Guard Rescue Coordination Center designated the *Mackinaw* the scene commander. On land, about one hundred volunteers walked the shoreline, looking for *Morrell* victims or wreckage that might have washed in.

Over the next few days, until December 3, when the active search and rescue mission was officially terminated, those scouring the lake for any

A lost *Morrell* crewman is carried off the *Acacia*. One of the airmen involved in the search stated, "That water was terrible. It was cold and full of death." Photograph by Ralph Polovich, Port Huron *Times Herald*.

signs of the *Morrell* had to battle rough weather and sailing conditions. Gale-force winds and blizzard snowfalls hampered their efforts. Blinding snowfall grounded the aircraft for significant periods. Air temperatures plummeted. Nine inches of ice formed on two 40-foot lifeboats, making them impossible to launch.

Dennis Miller, onboard the *Acacia*, would have nightmares about some of the work. On the first night of the search, he assisted with the spotlight as the *Acacia* dealt with heavy swells still rolling the boats as they made their way across the water. It was very cold, and, as Miller recalled, "steam was coming off the lake." The spotlight playing off all this cast an eerie light on the water. At one point, they saw what they determined to be a victim in a life jacket floating on the water, but the weather conditions, darkness, and process of maneuvering in the choppy waves made him impossible to recover.

"Night searches tend to be very unsuccessful," Charles Millradt, commander of the *Acacia*, allowed. It was difficult enough to catch anything on the water with the searchlight, he said; in these conditions, a victim or a shipwreck's flotsam could disappear between waves when the light was passing over the area. A boat in front of them dropped flares on the water to assist with the vision, but the flares were of little help.

Things were going no better onboard the *Bramble*. The 180-foot Coast Guard cutter struggled to keep its head to the sea, while her crew tried to remain upright as they searched for *Morrell* survivors. Roland Schultz, the *Bramble*'s quartermaster, estimated that half of the crew were too seasick to function, while the other half barely hung on. Outside the pilothouse, ice covered everything on deck. Men took turns standing a brief watch on the flying bridge, where they were tied in place to avoid their being swept overboard. After their watches, they were so encased in ice that "they looked like the Pillsbury doughboy." The searchlights played off the massive waves, while a fixed-wing aircraft dropped flares that stayed lit, even as they sank beneath the surface of the lake. "It was eerie," Schultz recalled.

Like Millradt, Schultz wondered what could have been done if they had seen Hale's raft or survivors in the water. Maneuvering the *Bramble* into a position where a rescue could have been attempted would have been almost impossible, and even if the cutter had actually moved into a position near someone in the water, the roiling waters might have caused the *Bramble* to crush the raft or run a man through the propeller. "It was just too dangerous," Schultz said.

When *Acacia* did start bringing in bodies, Miller found the work very hard to witness. The deck crew of the *Acacia*, experienced in hooking and tending to buoys, would send out a grappling hook and hope it caught a piece of clothing or life jacket on a body in the water. Some of the bodies were already in poor shape from the time they had been in the water and from seagulls picking at them. They would be hauled in, painstakingly lifted onboard the Coast Guard cutter, and placed on the boat's deck, where they would stay, covered with tarps. When the *Acacia* returned to Harbor Beach, the victims were gathered and driven to the funeral home by trucks and ambulances waiting dockside.

The boats used a grid pattern in their search, which ultimately covered four hundred square miles of Lake Huron. At 4:00 p.m. on the first day, almost exactly the same time that Hale's life raft was spotted by the Coast Guard helicopters, seven bodies were recovered by two helicopters and one of the smaller lifeboats. The bodies, as determined later, had drifted south about twelve miles from where the bow section had sunk.

The first victims found and identified (Captain Arthur Crawley, First Mate Phillip Kapets, Second Mate Duncan MacLeod, Wheelsman Stuart

The terrible toll of the *Morrell* tragedy was seen dockside in Harbor Beach, as lost sailors were loaded into awaiting ambulances and hearses and taken to the town's two funeral parlors and to makeshift morgues. Photograph by Ralph Polovich, Port Huron *Times Herald*.

Campbell, Wheelsman Henry Rischmiller, Watchman Albert Whoeme, Watchman Norman Bragg, and Ordinary Deckwatch Larry Davis) had worked and bunked in the front of the *Morrell*; at least some of them had been on the raft, awaiting the sinking of the ship, with Hale. All wore life jackets, and all were probably flung into the water with Hale. When testifying at the Coast Guard Board of Inquiry, Lynn Harivel, Bethlehem Steel's fleet engineer, estimated that twelve of the twenty-nine men onboard the *Morrell* would have been stationed in the bow section of the boat; if that estimation was correct, two-thirds of the forward crew, as well as Hale, had been recovered.

❯ ❯ ❯

Nurses awakened Hale a few times during his first night in the hospital, checking his temperature and other vital signs. They packed hot water bottles around him, and his temperature slowly began to rise. He warmed to 97.4 degrees within an hour and a half of his admittance to the hospital, and his temperature rocketed until it topped off at 101 degrees before

LAST EDITION

PORT HURON TIMES HERALD

WEATHER
Much Colder.
Snow Flurries.

THREE SECTIONS

PORT HURON, MICHIGAN, THURSDAY, DECEMBER 1, 1966

PRICE 10 CENTS

Survivor Tells Of Ordeal

DENNIS HALE

Other Stories, Pictures Of Ship Disaster On Pages 20A, 21A

Freighter With 29 Sinks Off Thumb; One Crewman Rescued

RAFT FROM WHICH CREWMAN WAS RESCUED

This is the raft from the sunken freighter Daniel J. Morrell from which crewman Dennis Hale, 26, Ashtabula, O., was rescued at 3:45 p.m. Wednesday by a Coast Guard helicopter from Traverse City as Hale of Harbor Beach. The bodies of Hale's three companions were still in the raft when Times Herald photographers Ralph W. Polovich took this aerial photo in a U.S. Air plane from the St. Clair County

HARBOR BEACH — Twenty-eight men apparently lost their lives when the 600-foot Bethlehem Steel company freighter Daniel J. Morrell broke up and sank in a vicious Lake Huron storm some 18 miles northeast of here early Tuesday.

A lone survivor was plucked at 3:45 p.m. Wednesday from his bobbing life raft as he asked with three dead companions. Nine more lifejacketed bodies have been picked up from the Lake. Virtually no hope is held that any more survivors will be found.

* * *

THE SURVIVOR, Dennis Hale, 26, Ashtabula, O., is recovering in Harbor Beach Community Hospital after a massive, 36-hour ordeal aboard the life raft.

His survival — the water temperature was about 35 and the air temperature dipped to the low 20's — is attributed to his 220-pound bulk and the fact that he buried himself in the raft underneath the bodies of his companions.

The body of one area crewman is among those of five identified so far; a second area resident aboard the vessel is presumed lost.

The body of Charles Henry Fosbender, 42, a wheelsman, of 713 Royal Street, St. Clair, was identified Wednesday night. Still missing is deckhand Clare G. Haley, 33, a former Port Huron area resident who listed his postoffice address as 7302 Laurel, Lexington Heights, Albert Dange, who lives at the Laurel Street address and, however, that Mr. Haley hadn't lived there for nearly two years.

Coast Guard vessels and helicopters resumed their search of the waters off Harbor Beach this morning and ground searchers checked the shoreline for 25 miles between Port Austin and Harbor

Beach in the hopes of finding more bodies or pieces of wreckage.

The search had been abandoned temporarily at 3:30 a.m. today to avail daylight. Snow fell in the area this morning, hampering search operations. The water temperature in that section of the Lake was reported at 33 to 40 degrees and the air temperature was 22. Zero readings are forecast for tonight.

THE MORRELL'S loss was recorded by the storm in 700 fathom — from 11:45 a.m. Tuesday when she transmitted a routine message giving her position as 24 miles north of Harbor Beach and 1:15 p.m. Wednesday when the vessel crossed U.S. Post spotted and recovered a lifejacketed body in the Lake between Harbor Beach and Port Hope.

Only two hours before that search, though the freighter Townsend passed the Morrell and saw nothing wrong, according to the freighter's captain, Joseph Frick.

A day and a half later, shortly after the Post spotted the first body, the Townsend found three more bodies floating in the Lake.

"All had no life jackets on with Morrell markings. They were in a degree of about a mile," Captain

John Brennan, a legal representative of the Bethlehem Steel company which operated the ill-fated Morrell, said with a total of 29 crewmen were aboard, including the captain, Arthur I. Crawley.

Continued on Page 20A, Col. 1

CHARLES H. FOSBENDER

Identify Body Of Fosbender In Ship Loss

(Related Story on Page 20A)

ST. CLAIR — Positive identification was made late Wednesday of the body of Charles H. Fosbender, 42, of 713 Royal Street, a wheelsman on the freighter Daniel J. Morrell.

Mr. Fosbender's body was recovered Wednesday during search operations.

MR. FOSBENDER was born July 31, 1924 in Port Huron, son of the late Anthony and Viola Fosbender. He and Janice Esry were married Nov. 30, 1957.

He is survived by his widow; three daughters, Francis McMahon, Antoinette, a stepdaughter, Mrs. Shirley Bradley; Diane, Mich.; two sisters, Mrs. Lora Oberbrekling, Indiana, and Mrs. Ruth Harrington, Port Huron.

CLARE C. HALEY

Thumb Area Resident Is Among Missing

Clare C. Haley, 33, one of the missing crewmen of the Daniel J. Morrell, is a former Port Huron area resident who lived for several years in the Croswell area. Residents at that address said, however, that Haley hadn't lived there for nearly two years.

STARTING FRIDAY

Old Newsboys To Sell Papers

The fortieth annual Old Newsboys association sale will be held Friday and Saturday in Port Huron.

Veteran newsboys with a special edition of The Times Herald to area residents do whatever price they are able will bring to give.

The worthwhile accomplishing this article has the various locations by the Old Newsboys sellers. The cash will be held from 1 to 9 p.m. Friday and from 1 to 5 p.m. Saturday.

Funds collected by the newsboys will be divided by the Old

Day's is proof to buy sheets, Old Newsboys. With the help of funds, stockings and underwear quarters and shirts to schoolchildren in the counties in care of The Times Herald. Some groups need donations from these own families.

During the last 40 years, activities netted nearly $130,000 which have been donated $100,000 for the transportation have donated $150,000 by the Newsboys affiliates.

With these funds, 9,165 children received 3,537 different blankets have been helped.

Items purchased:
16,860 pairs of shoes.
16,810 pairs of hose.
23,500 pairs of underwear.
28,800 pairs of underwear.
And 640 suits of socks. Last year, was the first time boxes were included.

Where To Find It

Local News	1-5
District News	8C
Ann Landers	8-C
Churches	9
Classified	3-5
Dr. Molner	2
Family Living	4, 5, 8
Markets	4
Sports	6, 7
Theaters	2
School News	2D, 10A
TV Previews	2
Vitally	2
Want Ads	2, 5

Weather Forecast

(Weather Map on Page 20A)

Port Huron Area — Much colder tonight with occasional snow flurries, the probable low temperature 8-12 degrees. Mist to northwest winds 12-18 miles diminishing a little. Considerable cloudiness and cool Friday. Partial cloudiness and colder. Saturday night snow flurries. Wintry cold. Probable high near 30 degrees Friday.

TEMPERATURES			
Highest			
30 — 4:50 a.m. Yesterday		35 — Noon Today	
Lowest			
32 — 8 p.m. Yesterday		29 — 6 a.m. Today	
Yesterday		Today	
1 p.m.	35	1 a.m.	33
4 p.m.	35	4 a.m.	31
7 p.m.	34	7 a.m.	30
10 p.m.	33	10 a.m.	31
Midnight	33	Noon	35

Today's Chuckle

A beauty contest could prove aptly be termed the last roundup.

adjusting to normal temperature. As famished as he was, Hale was unable to keep any food down.

The hospital managed to keep the news media away from him, but Hale understood that he would have to talk to reporters in the near future. He hated the thought. The *Morrell* story was front-page news in area papers, and interest in it was growing. As the wreck's sole survivor, he was at the center of the story. The public was bestowing hero status on him, but he saw himself in an entirely different light. He conceded that his survival was amazing, but in his mind there was nothing heroic about it. He had survived circumstances beyond his control. As far as he was concerned, the media should have concentrated on his missing or lost crewmates.

Hale faced what he would be seeing in the future during his first full day in the hospital when he was visited by Art Dobson, the Cleveland dispatcher for Bethlehem Steel, and two Coast Guard officers. No one yet knew anything about the sinking of the *Morrell*, other than the fact that victims and wreckage had been picked up. How and when the *Morrell* sank were mysteries. Hale spent an hour and a half with the three men, talking about the storm, the *Morrell*'s breaking apart, and, most difficult for him, his survival on the raft. Hale held his patience, but he had no interest in retelling his story. It was too painful.

It was more of the same when he met the media the next day. He had never been interviewed, with the exception of his meeting with Dobson and the two others from the Coast Guard, and he was frightened by the prospects of having his words recorded for newspapers and magazines. He wasn't sure of what was expected of him. He had been contacted earlier about a telephone interview for Joe Pyne's popular but controversial Los Angeles television program; hospital personal had advised him against taking the call.

Then he was visited again by Father McEachin, who further clouded his mind about what information he should be volunteering to reporters. Hale wanted to talk to the priest about his spiritual experiences on the raft, most particularly Doc and the vision of the afterlife. If anyone could understand his experiences and the joy he felt over them, it would be this man. Hale wanted to address these experiences when he talked to the press, but McEachin surprised him with his response to the idea.

"Oh, Dennis, I don't think you should talk about that," he advised.

Hale hid his disappointment, but he was deeply hurt by the priest's remark. Hale considered himself a religious man; his faith demanded that he believe in spiritual matters much deeper than anything he had experienced on the raft. But here he was, seeking counsel from someone who might have understood some of the most important events in his life and being told, in essence, that people would think he was crazy if he mentioned what had happened to him.

"I had more to tell him about the strange things that happened to me," Hale wrote later in his autobiography, "but when he said that, I listened to him and didn't say another word. He made me feel ashamed and unclean and that people might think I was a little deranged."

"People are afraid of brains," Dr. Robert Oakes observed, adding that what Hale had experienced was delirium. Oakes believed that the hallucinations, along with Hale's religious faith, "most likely pulled him through." This wasn't dementia or depression, but a positive, comforting experience—one that Hale needed in a life-threatening situation.

After McEachin left, Hale decided that for as long as he lived, he would never publicly discuss these experiences.

His bed was wheeled out of his room and into the presence of a couple dozen reporters and television cameras. He was joined by his wife, Bertha, who had flown in earlier in the day with his stepmother and stepbrother. The circumstances were far from ideal: the *Morrell* story was still breaking, and reporters had to write articles about the ship's sinking, Hale's survival, the search for survivors, and anything else that might be pertinent. Deadlines for that evening's papers were tight.

For the second time in as many days, Hale offered his account of the sinking and his survival. He also spoke briefly about his past, of his work as a chef, and how he came to work on the freighters. Bertha told reporters that her husband had always been terrified of storms, that they had talked about his leaving the lakes for employment on land.

"There just wasn't anything else available as far as money and jobs," she said.

Hale volunteered nothing about his out-of-body experiences, other than to mention that he had had hallucinations. One of the most riveting moments rose from his describing his conversation with Father McEachin.

"Father, why am I here?" he had asked.

"You are here because God wanted you to be alive," the priest answered.

When talking to reporters, Hale offered two explanations for why he was alive.

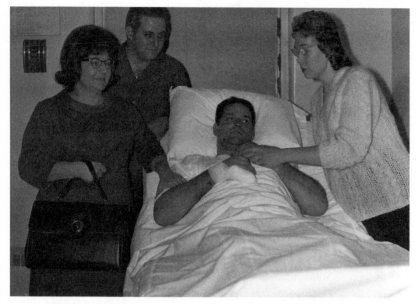

Dennis Hale is visited by his stepmother, Cecilia, his brother Louis, and his wife, Bertha, in his Harbor Beach hospital room. Photograph by Ralph Polovich, Port Huron *Times Herald*.

"First, perhaps God wants me to be alive," Hale said. "And secondly, perhaps God wants me to suffer before I die."

The statement became one of the most quoted offerings in the interview. When the newspaper accounts of the interview were published, Hale's initial reservations about meeting with the press proved to have been valid. There were errors in virtually every account. Some stories had Hale sharing the raft with Captain Crawley, First Mate Phillip Kapets, and Second Mate Duncan MacLeod, even though the bodies of all three had been picked up by the *Acacia* the previous day and Hale had identified the three crewmates on the raft. The reports could not agree on the number of officers and crewmen onboard; Bethlehem Steel finally set the number straight. In almost every account Hale was said to have burrowed beneath the bodies of his dead shipmates for warmth—a statement Hale vigorously denied later.

> > >

While Hale was engaged with the media in Harbor Beach, one of his crewmates, Hjalmer Edwards, was talking about the *Morrell* from a War

Memorial Hospital bed in Sault Ste. Marie. Like others before him in maritime history, Edwards should have been onboard a shipwrecked vessel but was spared when left his vessel just before her final trip.

The sixty-one-year-old Edwards came from a line of Swedish American mariners working on fishing boats. He had operated his own fishing boat in his youth and knew the fickle moods of Great Lakes weather: he had lost his boat in a Lake Superior storm. He also learned, from extensive hardscrabble experience, about the difficulties of earning a living as a commercial fisherman. He had left the business for the more stable life in commercial shipping. Prior to working on the *Morrell*, the Superior, Wisconsin, sailor had worked as a chief steward for the Columbia and Hutchinson lines. He had been employed on the *C. G. Post*, the freighter that found the first *Morrell* victim.

He had worked on the *Daniel J. Morrell* since September, and he listed porter Joseph Mahsem and watchman Albert Whoeme as good friends.

He did not know Hale.

"I'd know him if I saw his picture," he told reporters. "In the galley we called everyone by their first names, Pete, Joe, Nick, George, or what have you."

The captain and first mate, he said, had been capable sailors, and the morale on the *Morrell* had been good. The *Morrell* handled rough seas well, at least in his limited experience on her, and she must have sunk very quickly if she hadn't had time to send an SOS.

"That's a nasty stretch of sea there in heavy weather, and I'm glad I wasn't there," he said.

"I've been shipwrecked before and know what it's like to come busting in on the rollers. It happened up on Lake Superior when I owned my own fish tug and it got wrecked in a storm."

He had left the *Morrell* on Thanksgiving, only days before she sank, when he developed pneumonia from a bad cold. He had a survivor's mixed feelings when he was shown a crew list. He mourned a loss while feeling extremely lucky to be alive.

"If I hadn't gotten off at the Sault on Thanksgiving Day, I'd have had it," he reflected. "I'm awfully glad I wasn't on her, of course, but I feel terrible about all those other poor fellows, many of whom I knew well."

> > >

The 180-foot Coast Guard cutter *Acacia* continued to search for survivors, but no one other than Dennis Hale was found alive. Photograph by Ralph Polovich, Port Huron *Times Herald*.

The second day of searching for survivors commenced early in the morning. Before the day ended, another nine bodies were recovered from the lake. All were from the *Morrell's* stern. Three had been seen floating on the choppy water shortly after the day's search began. They were picked up by the *Mackinaw* and *Acacia*. Six more bodies were removed from the water by the *Acacia* shortly before two in the afternoon. That meant that twenty-one of the crew, including Hale, were accounted for.

The bodies were brought to Harbor Beach and divided between the city's two funeral homes. Identifying the victims, a grisly chore under the best of circumstances, was made more difficult when Bethlehem Steel initially balked at supplying a crew list. Forty-eight hours earlier, the steel company owners had assumed that all was well, that the *Morrell* was sailing toward Taconite Harbor for a load of iron ore. Now it was dealing with the loss of a vessel and her crew, the cold fact that in all probability twenty-eight men would have to be identified and their families notified, and the inevitability of lawsuits and a full-scale investigation about causes and responsibility for the vessel's loss. What was the protocol for all this?

Regardless of the answer to the question, the owners and operators of the *Morrell* erred in not immediately notifying the crewmen's families of the *Morrell's* sinking as soon as they knew the vessel had been lost. Instead, families learned of the tragedy elsewhere. Cecilia Stojek was washing her lunch dishes when she heard a radio report saying that the *Morrell* had sunk; she collapsed on the spot. The Cleary family, fresh from a birthday party for John's ten-year-old sister the night the *Morrell* sank, received a call asking John Sr. to come to Harbor Beach; a body resembling his son had been recovered from a raft. Jan Fosbender, who had just received a letter from her husband the day he was found dead on the raft, sat by a radio with friends and awaited additional news about the *Morrell*. She knew nothing about the discovery of her husband's body, and she allowed herself a faint hope when word of a survivor came in. The next day, the name of that survivor appeared in newspapers everywhere.

The *Morrell's* crew list was released by Bethlehem Steel when the FBI dispatched agents with fingerprint files to Harbor Beach. A print of each body's right index finger was taken, and the FBI looked for a match. One by one, the bodies were identified, and the victim's family was notified. Those recovered on the second day included Chief Engineer John Schmidt, First Assistant Engineer Valmour Marchildon, Fireman Chester Konieczka, Fireman Arthur Fargo, Oiler Wilson Simpson, Coal Passer Leon Truman, Second Cook Nicholas Homick, Porter Joseph Mahsem, and Porter Charles Sestakauskas.

One of the most bizarre stories to rise out of the search and rescue operations began on the first day. A Coast Guard helicopter spied what appeared to be an unoccupied raft caught in the rocks near Pointe Aux Barques, but because they could see no survivors or victims on the raft, the helicopter pilots reasoned that the raft could be recovered at another time. They reported their discovery and resumed their search.

That same day, Huron City resident Earl Gudakunst saw the same raft about a half mile offshore of his property. He and a friend, Ken Schave, decided to investigate. They took Gudakunst's fishing boat to the raft. Not only had they located the *Morrell's* stern life raft, but upon closer inspection they saw a crewman's foot poking out from beneath the raft. The two men pulled a life-jacketed man as far as they could from beneath the raft. He had been wedged between the pontoons. The two men secured the dead sailor to the raft with a rope, headed back to shore, and called the sheriff. The sheriff, in turn, contacted the Coast Guard. They were aware of the raft, the Coast Guard told the sheriff, but they knew nothing about a body. They would retrieve it as soon as possible.

Somehow, in all the frenetic search and rescue activities, the gathering

Life rings and life vests were among the few things recovered after the *Morrell's* sinking. Courtesy of the Pointe Aux Barques Lighthouse Society.

of victims, the rescue of Hale (that same afternoon), and the retrieval of flotsam from the *Morrell*, the stern's life raft was forgotten. Nearly five full days passed before the corpse and raft were picked up. The body was identified as George Dahl, the *Morrell's* third assistant engineer. His retrieval set off a volley of speculation about the raft: perhaps others had been on it as well—signs that someone had escaped the sinking stern—but there was no indication of it. All of the raft's emergency equipment—the flare gun, the flares, the oil can, and sea anchor—were still stored away, unused.

When the search officially ended on December 5, Hale and twenty-one of his deceased crewmen had been picked up. Hale's Ashtabula friend, Saverio Grippi, would be found all the way across the lake in Tiverton, Ontario, on December 10, but no one else would turn up until the following spring. On April 15, oiler Don Worcester's remains were found near Southhampton, Ontario; the next day, the badly decomposed remains of Ernie Marcotte, the *Morrell's* third mate, would turn up in the same area.

Two men would never be recovered: Steward Stanley Satlawa and Deckhand John Groh, who had ridden with Hale to catch the *Morrell* in Windsor after they had missed the boat in Lackawanna. Two additional men, Coal Passer David Price and Second Assistant Engineer Alfred Norkunas, would be found near the end of May.

Hale tried to keep track of the search efforts from his hospital bed in Harbor Beach. He held out hope that someone would be found alive, but he was finally told that time and weather conditions had made it impossible for others to have survived. Aside from some life jackets, life rings, oars, two life rafts, and a small amount of wreckage found in the water or on shore, Hale was all that remained of the *Daniel J. Morrell*.

The *Daniel J. Morrell* appears here in much calmer waters than those on the night of November 29. Painting by Robert McGreevy. Courtesy of the artist.

PUBLIC AUTOPSY

THE COAST GUARD HEARINGS

A FLURRY OF ACTIVITY FOLLOWED THE LOSS OF THE *DANIEL J. Morrell*, the rescue of Dennis Hale, and the failure to find more crewmen alive. The recovery of lost seamen meant the planning of funerals, even as the search for other victims continued. The families of the lost, shipping authorities, the press, the general public—all demanded answers. It seemed inconceivable that two huge freighters had split and sunk, with only three survivors, over a period of less than a decade. Why had it taken so long for the *Morrell* to be reported as missing? Why, for that matter, had there been no distress signal? Was the *Morrell*—and other older vessels working on the lakes late in the shipping season—antiquated? Who was to blame?

Whenever there was a shipwreck with loss of life, the Coast Guard assembled a board of inquiry to answer these and other questions. On December 2, Admiral Willard J. Smith announced from his Washington, D.C., base that he was appointing a five-member board to study the loss of the *Daniel J. Morrell*. He correctly anticipated a flood of lawsuits to be filed against the owners and operators of the *Morrell*, and when assembling the board, he saw that it would be made up of the best officers he could gather. Leading the panel would be Rear Admiral Charles Tighe, the highly regarded commander of the Ninth Coast Guard District, headquartered in Cleveland.

Meanwhile, the tiny Michigan city of Harbor Beach prepared to honor the *Morrell*'s lost crew members. An interfaith memorial service conducted by Catholic, Presbyterian, and Baptist clergy was scheduled for Tuesday, December 6, at Our Lady of Lake Huron Church. It would be an official day of mourning, with schools closing at noon and all stores closed from two to three that afternoon. On the day of the service, a single empty casket, draped in black and symbolizing all those lost in the *Morrell* tragedy, stood at the front of the church, while the clergymen spoke solemnly about the way the loss of the sailors profoundly affected people who didn't even know them. "Any one of us might have been able to say, 'one of the men on the *Daniel J. Morrell* was my father, my brother, my son,'" said Rev. David J. Miller.

Locating the wreckage of the *Daniel J. Morrell*, a top priority as soon as realistic hope for finding other survivors was abandoned, became a frustrating, time-consuming, expensive undertaking. Hopes rose when on December 2 two Coast Guard planes detected what they believed to be one of the submerged sections of the *Morrell* about twenty-six miles north of Harbor Beach, not far from where they had discovered a portion of a broken lifeboat. It seemed promising, since broken oars and life jackets had also been found near Harbor Beach. They marked the location with a buoy and prepared for a closer examination.

The waiting game began. Rough weather delayed the exploration. Eight men had yet to be recovered, and their families anxiously awaited any news about the discovery of their remains. One of the missing, coal passer Saverio "Sam" Grippi, had been Hale's best friend in Ashtabula. Hale hunted with Grippi, and the Hales and Grippis got together for spaghetti dinners. Grippi's unknown status led to an awkward meeting when his wife and her sister visited Hale in the hospital. Sarah Grippi struggled with the fact that her husband had been lost while Hale had been rescued, a situation that caused Hale more suffering than any of his physical maladies.

Aside from its interest in locating the *Morrell* wreckage for answers it might provide its investigation, the Coast Guard had a practical reason for seeking the two sections of the boat: if the *Morrell* had sunk in shallow water and come to rest in an upright position—a common enough occurrence with shipwrecks—the wreckage might pose a hazard to other vessels passing through the area. Bethlehem Steel had similar concerns. The company had no plans for salvaging the wreck, but along with having the same questions about the *Morrell*'s demise as the Coast Guard, Bethlehem officials faced imposing settlements with the families of the lost sailors.

The press wanted any information it could get. Public interest in this latest shipwreck ran high, especially in the *Morrell*'s disappearance without a trace. The wreck had left virtually no evidence of her sinking—no oil slicks, as are common in shipwrecks, no large pieces of wreckage, only the terrible evidence of human loss—which only fed into the growing sense of mystery shrouding the story.

The inclement weather hinted of worse ahead. Portions of the lake were known to freeze over during the winter months, and no one wanted to suspend the search until the following spring. Then, to the mounting frustration of all involved, the mass discovered by the Coast Guard on December 2 turned out to be a false alarm. Bethlehem Steel contracted the McQueen Marine Company, an Ontario firm, to find and identify the wreck. Days passed. The bad weather held. After having no luck whatsoever between December 13 and December 20, the mission was abandoned.

> > >

On December 2, the same day that Admiral Smith was announcing the formation of the board of inquiry, Coast Guard inspectors boarded the *Edward Y. Townsend* to survey the storm's damage to the *Morrell's* sister ship.

Captain Thomas Connelly realized how fortunate he had been to sail to safety. After speaking to Arthur Crawley for the last time, Connelly fought his way through what he would call the worst storm he had ever encountered in his experiences on the lakes. He reached Lime Island and docked for refueling. Walking the *Townsend's* deck and checking for any damage the boat might have sustained in the maelstrom, he was shocked to discover a crack in the deck plates on the starboard side near the tenth hatch, starting at the hatch coaming and extending out toward the center of the boat. He had no way of knowing it then, but the sixteen-inch crack was in the same general area as the split in the *Morrell*.

Connelly alerted the Coast Guard of his discovery. His shipping season was over. As soon as Coast Guard inspectors visited the *Townsend* and saw the crack, the vessel's sailing certificate was pulled, meaning that no crew, cargo, or passengers were permitted to sail on the *Townsend* until further notice. Welders made temporary repairs, but the *Townsend* would need more extensive work before it sailed again. She was towed, first, to the Carbide dock in Sault Ste. Marie, Ontario, and, a short time later, to the Algoma Central Railway dock in Sault Ste. Marie.

The board of inquiry, hearing of the damage to the deck, ordered a thorough inspection.

"There are a number of similarities between the two ships," explained Robert Chirnside, an inspector with the Coast Guard Inspection Office in Detroit, and one of three inspectors assigned to give the *Townsend* a complete going over. The *Morrell* and *Townsend* had been identical but for 1 foot in length, sailing under identical conditions in the same storm, in the same area of Lake Huron. The *Morrell* had split in two, and by all appearances,

This dramatic sequence, photographed by a crew member aboard the Polish tug *Koral* on November 17, 1972, documents how the *Michipicoten*, a large freighter like the *Daniel J. Morrell*, broke apart and sank in stormy seas. The *Edward Y. Townsend*, while being towed across the Atlantic four years later, sank under similar conditions. Courtesy of Roger LeLievre, Great Lakes and Seaway Shipping On-Line, Inc.

the *Townsend* was in the process of doing the same. The three inspectors hoped to question Captain Connelly and some of his crew about the storm and how the *Townsend* responded to it.

"We are going to look at the crack and the general condition of the vessel in hopes this will tell us something," Chirnside said.

What they found only added to the confusion. The *Townsend*'s hull showed signs of stress, of the twisting and turning, the pitching and rolling, and the pounding she took from heavy winds and seas, but aside from the crack in the deck itself, the damage was inexplicably light.

"The metal in the midship area of the vessel, including deck, shell, internals and all structural members appeared to be in surprisingly good material condition," the Coast Guard reported in its final report on the loss of the *Morrell*, concluding that "the wear down or deterioration was considered negligible."

Any crack in the deck is very serious, but the inspectors were hard-pressed to explain how it got there: "Other than the normal stress corrosion, cracks and evidence of working rivets," the Coast Guard concluded, "there was nothing found that would explain the reason for the crack in the spar deck. Excluding the crack in the spar deck, no evidence of major structural weakness was found."

The fact that the crack was located in roughly the same place as the split eight years earlier on the *Carl D. Bradley* brought up some compelling questions. These questions would be raised during the board of inquiry hearings.

> > >

Attorneys always posed challenges to Coast Guard boards investigating a shipwreck when a loss of life had occurred. Lawyers representing shipping companies, the families of lost sailors, maritime unions, and other parties with a vested interest in the board's determinations would take seats in the hearing room, their ears trained on every word spoken by witnesses and experts testifying on what might have caused a disaster. A misspoken word could lead to a hefty exchange of money.

Victor G. Hanson, a Detroit attorney representing several families of crewmen lost on the *Daniel J. Morrell* and the Seafarers International Union, had worked on high-profile shipwreck cases prior to the *Morrell*, including the *Andrea Doria* (1956), a passenger liner that sank in the Atlantic

Ocean, leaving fifty-two dead; the *Carl D. Bradley* (1958), which claimed thirty-three lives; and most recently, the *Cedarville* (1965), which carried ten men to the bottom of the Straits of Mackinac after being broadsided by another vessel in the fog. Hanson would eventually become involved with the investigation of the loss of the *Edmund Fitzgerald* (1975), the most notorious (and recent) shipwreck in Great Lakes history, which took the lives of twenty-nine sailors after being caught in a furious storm on Lake Superior. Hanson not only knew maritime law but was also well versed in labor law. He would be an imposing presence in the Coast Guard hearings and the eventual court cases deciding lawsuits filed against the owners and operators of the *Morrell*.

Hanson was intrigued by the similarities between the *Bradley* and *Morrell* accidents. Both involved boats that had been caught in violent storms, both breaking in two and sinking quickly. In both cases, four men had escaped to a life raft, two surviving the *Bradley* sinking after spending a night on Lake Michigan, Hale the lone survivor of the *Morrell*. Most interesting, perhaps, was the fact that both vessels had been sailing without cargo, under ballast, which led to questions about their structural integrity. Since both were aging freighters built long before the beginning of the use of stronger, less brittle metals in hull construction, one could not help but wonder whether the *Morrell* and *Bradley* broke apart as the result of metal failure resulting from all the twisting they had taken in rough seas over the years, coupled with their steel becoming brittle in the cold water. If this proved to be the case, what could be done about the other freighters built before 1948? By the Coast Guard's count, there were 137 such boats working on the lakes in 1966, including the *Edward Y. Townsend*, which might have been spared only by good fortune.

"It seems in the past couple of decades, there's a sinking in the Great Lakes about every 10 years," Hanson told a reporter for the *Montreal Gazette*. "Sailing is a very dangerous job in November when the Great Lakes are treacherous, especially on ships that are nothing more than motorized barges."

Hanson listened intently to the testimony at the Coast Guard Board of Inquiry hearings, and he was not satisfied with what he heard. When Lynwood C. Harivel, Bethlehem Steel's fleet engineer, testified on December 5, the first day of hearings, that "there [was] nothing wrong" with the *Morrell* structurally, while conceding that the company's policy of inspecting its vessels' hulls was only visual, similar to Coast Guard inspections,

Hanson voiced a legitimate protest. How could Harivel so positively declare that there was nothing wrong with the *Morrell* when he did not test for metal fatigue, when he was not a metallurgist and did not actually conduct tests or use scientific methods in determining the strength of a hull?

Hanson was similarly displeased when the board of inquiry refused to admit as evidence a letter written on November 6 by *Morrell* coal passer Leon R. Truman to his wife. "The fog lifted about 7 a.m. this morning so we could get into the dock," Truman wrote. "Two more tubes blew in the boiler. This old boat has just about had it." Truman's observations, along with other complaints about the boat's condition, registered in letters by others, were, the board ruled, "hearsay evidence."

Aside from his assertion that the Coast Guard used out-of-date technology in its inspection of a boat, Hanson objected to the composition of the board of inquiry itself. It was a "whitewash," he fumed, a matter of the Coast Guard investigating itself. After all, it had been the Coast Guard that had inspected the *Morrell* and deemed it seaworthy. Now, in the aftermath of that boat's hull failure and the loss of twenty-eight lives, the Coast Guard was conducting a hearing in which it might have to rule that it might have been mistaken, that the *Morrell* might not have been seaworthy after all. Hanson was further rankled by the way the hearings were conducted. Lawyers for Bethlehem Steel was permitted to question witnesses called before the board, but Hanson and attorneys representing unions or the men lost in the sinking were only allowed to submit written questions to be vetted by the board, which then decided whether they should be used in the proceedings. He had had this experience in the *Bradley* hearings, the refusal coming on the grounds of the hearings not being a trial.

The ruling was similar now with the *Morrell*.

"You have the privilege of being an interested party," Tighe told Hanson in a ruling made on the first day of the hearings, "but not a party of interest."

As a result of the ruling, Hanson and other attorneys submitted eighty-seven written questions, many highly technical, for Harivel alone.

Hanson, a Marine Corps veteran who had earned his law degree at Wayne State University, opposed the practice of having shipwreck investigations conducted only by the Coast Guard. It would be better, he proposed, to include representatives from the Department of Commerce and the Department of Justice. Drawing conclusions based on the evidence and testimony at the hearings, as well as acting on those conclusions, might be more fair to all concerned if there was a wider range of interests seated on the boards of inquiry.

Tighe strongly disagreed with Hanson's charges of a "whitewash" proceeding. "I am most anxious to determine the cause of the accident," he declared. "I am not interested in protecting the company or any member of the Coast Guard."

Tighe did eventually back off his written questions ruling; attorneys representing the unions or the families of lost sailors would be allowed to verbally direct their questions to witnesses.

> > >

In cases like the *Daniel J. Morrell*, where a vessel was lost in a storm, there was customarily an intense focus on a captain's decision to sail. His decision was final. After the sinking of the *Carl D. Bradley*, the Coast Guard board concluded that Captain Roland Bryan "exercised poor judgment" in his decision to sail. "This decision," the Coast Guard's final report read, "was probably by zealous desire to hold as closely to schedule as possible, and because of this, he gave less attention to the dangers of the existing weather than what might be expected of a prudent mariner."

Captain Arthur Crawley's actions were under similar scrutiny. Michigan had been battered by a storm prior to Crawley's arrival on Lake Huron. On the evening of November 27, rather than sail in deteriorating weather conditions, Crowley had anchored the *Morrell* overnight near Detroit. The next day, despite forecasts of gale conditions, he had taken the *Morrell* out. Had he exercised poor judgment in making his decision to head out in what was certain to be a difficult run? Crawley admitted as much when he was seated on the raft just before the sinking of the bow portion of the *Morrell*. But this regret, of course, was hindsight expressed under extreme circumstances. His decision to sail had been based on his faith in his vessel: she had passed inspections before and during the current shipping season; she had a long history of handling inclement, even extreme weather, including the storm that brought down the *Carl D. Bradley*.

The Coast Guard's judgments concerning Crawley's actions were crucial. Six-figure lawsuits, filed by the victims' next of kin, were piling up. On December 8, Hale filed a suit seeking $150,000, his claim saying the *Morrell* was unseaworthy at the time of the sinking. The boat, he asserted, had shown structural deterioration in rust and corrosion. Hale further alleged that Bethlehem Steel failed to provide adequate repairs and emergency equipment. As the only witness and survivor of the sinking, Hale's testimony before the board of inquiry would bear heavy weight in the board's judgment and in legal action against Bethlehem Steel.

The debate centered on the strength of the storm and Captain Crawley's actions versus the condition of the *Morrell* and her safety features. A parade of testimony before the board led to further controversy. Lieutenant Richard C. Tims, one of the Toledo Coast Guard inspectors examining the *Morrell* in February 1966, noted that rivets and plates had been replaced during the *Morrell's* layup over the winter, and despite protests from Bethlehem Steel, supports on the starboard side were fortified to his satisfaction. He did not second-guess his giving the *Morrell* a clean bill of health.

Frank D. Brian, a thirty-eight-year veteran of Great Lakes sailing now employed by Bethlehem Steel, recalled crawling around the vessel's side and double-bottom tanks, checking for structural problems but finding nothing. "I did not see any deteriorated rivets, metal, brackets, frames, or distorted metal of any kind," he testified. "I would have remembered this distinctly."

Thomas Burns, the *Morrell's* third mate until August 1966, said the freighter was in good condition at the time of his leaving her. The *Morrell* did take water through the hull, he admitted, but added, "that's common with all the lakers." The captain, he said, was the one making the decision to sail, but Crawley, from his experience and what he had heard, had "a good reputation."

William Hull, the *Morrell's* master until Crawley took over in August 1966, supported Burns's and Brian's testimony. Like Brian, he had seen very little indication of problems with deterioration of metal or with rivets. He certainly did not see the estimated two hundred to five hundred leaky rivets that Harvey Hayes, another *Morrell* crewman, testified that he had seen during the 1965 shipping season. There might have been a half dozen bad rivets prior to the 1966 season, Hull said, and those had been repaired. The *Morrell*, he declared, was in good condition up until the end of his time on the boat. Eight years earlier, he had been second mate on the *Morrell* when, sailing on Lake Superior, the boat plowed through the storm that destroyed the *Carl D. Bradley*. That storm, Hull testified, had generated greater wind velocity and bigger waves. It had taken eighteen hours to sail forty-five miles, but the *Morrell* had come through the storm unscathed.

There was very little disagreement about the severity of the storm that brought down the *Daniel J. Morrell*. One by one, captains of freighters spoke of the difficulties they had battling the storm. All agreed that it would have been impossible to launch a lifeboat in such heavy winds and waves. When Thomas Connelly offered his account of the storm, he spoke of encountering "confused seas"—waves coming from two directions at once—that pounded and rolled the *Edward Y. Townsend*. By his estimation, he had talked to Captain Crawley on seven occasions about the weather and his plans for sailing in it. "I might have mentioned to Crawley I was thinking of turning back," Connelly told the board. The winds were increasing, and the heavy seas continued to build by the hour. Connelly recalled his abbreviated call from Crawley at 11:50 p.m. on November 28, how he had told the *Morrell* captain that he was busy in the pilothouse, trying to keep the *Townsend* on course. Less than a half hour later, at 12:15, Connelly returned the call, and Crawley mentioned that he, too, was struggling to keep his vessel from being blown off course. "The conversation was quite brief," Connelly said. "I just wished him luck."

It was the last time the two captains spoke.

❯ ❯ ❯

Hale was eager to leave the hospital in Harbor Beach. His physical condition required more medical attention than he would be receiving at his home, but there was no reason to believe he couldn't return to Ashtabula and receive adequate treatment in a hospital in his hometown. The holiday season was coming up soon, and while Hale was enjoying his celebrity status, with all the special attention he was receiving from the hospital staff, the write-ups in the newspapers, and the posing for bedside photographs, he wanted to be closer to his family. A decision was reached to transfer him to the Ashtabula General Hospital.

He was taken by ambulance. He had not been outside since the day of his rescue, and he brooded when he saw Lake Huron under a familiar gray sky.

"I [could] almost hear the lake talking to me and telling me that it missed me this time ... but there will be another time," he would say.

As the Ramsey Funeral Home ambulance made its way south, Hale learned how extensive the news of his survival had traveled. Cars pulled up alongside the ambulance, and drivers honked their horns and waved. It was more of the same when the ambulance delivered him to the hospital in Ashtabula. In the weeks to follow, everybody Hale knew seemed to drop by for a visit, and the press was just as interested in hearing his story as it had been in Michigan. He was torn by all the attention: he was pleased to be celebrated for his survival, but it meant being continually reminded of the price his fellow shipmates had paid in the *Morrell*'s sinking.

> > >

On December 23, Hale offered the board of inquiry his highly anticipated account of the *Morrell* sinking and his ordeal on the raft. He had already talked briefly to the press from his hospital beds in Harbor Beach and Ashtabula, but now he was expected to answer a battery of questions in as much detail as he could remember—and he could vividly recall almost everything that happened except, oddly enough, exactly how he had wound up in the water. He could describe his plunge beneath the icy waves of Lake Huron, his popping back to the surface and frantically swimming for the raft, the torturous hours adrift, the deaths of his crewmates, and his eventual rescue, but he struggled to remember anything about the wave that washed him overboard.

The board of inquiry, although interested in Hale's survival story, was for the purpose of its investigation mainly concerned with the events leading up to and including the *Morrell*'s sinking. Hale dreaded the thought of answering so many questions. The interviews in the hospitals had been difficult enough. Those asking the questions did not seem to understand his physical condition or mental anguish. When he was taken from the raft and transported to the hospital in Harbor Beach, he had been physically, psychologically, and emotionally wounded. In the weeks that passed between the rescue and two days before Christmas, he had recovered slowly but only partially. He still could not walk. The pain and pinprick sensations in his legs and feet had largely subsided, but he continued to suffer discomfort. When he tried to stand, he felt as if his legs were filling with fluid. As he would eventually learn, he had sustained serious nerve damage requiring time and rest to heal.

His mental and emotional distress was worse. His relief in surviving was tempered by the terrible knowledge that he was the only *Morrell* crew member to do so. Why, he asked himself, had he lived? Was there somehow a greater purpose or meaning to his life? For answers, he looked to a higher power. Raised Catholic, he was accustomed to praying; on the raft, however, he had also been angry with his God. He had prayed for death. Then, in the hospital, the priest had advised him to say nothing about what he felt were powerful spiritual experiences on the raft. Talking to the press, with all the questions about his survival, only reinforced his confusion. Much of what he thought about began with the word *why*.

After his conversations with the priest and his experiences with the press, Hale would have preferred to say nothing further, but here was the board of inquiry, trying to solve the mystery of the *Daniel J. Morrell's* sinking, asking him to relive his experiences. He knew nothing about the Coast Guard's boards of inquiry as standard procedure following the sinking of a boat involving loss of life. He was nervous in the days preceding his testimony.

The Coast Guard board, as well as attorneys representing Bethlehem Steel and the families of the victims and members of the press, traveled to Ashtabula to interview Hale at the hospital. His hospital bed was wheeled into a fifth-floor conference room, and with his wife nearby, Hale answered every question posed and even volunteered explanations and information not included in the questioning. His overall testimony took portions of a day and a half. The line of questioning was aimed not only to shed light on how and why the *Morrell* had broken apart but also to seek any clues to where the vessel's wreckage might be located. Hale told his story from the beginning through his dramatic rescue. His account accentuated just how long he had suffered during his ordeal on the lake: "After an hour or two hours my legs froze and I couldn't move them," he told those gathered by his bed.

The Coast Guard board members pressed Hale for his observations about the condition of the *Morrell* prior to the storm, and it was here that he offered some of his most compelling testimony. The freighter, he said, "leaked like a sieve," mainly due to what he estimated to be a thousand bad rivets.

"There has never been a time since I have been sailing that there's never been any holes in it," he said. "The port side has been getting worse right along. It was always leaky and had to be pumped out." He estimated that 25 percent of the rivets in the hold were bad.

Hale further stated that he would not have signed on to the *Morrell* for the 1966 season had he known of her condition; he assumed that the

Morrell, after been worked on the previous winter and then passing Coast Guard inspections, was in good shape for sailing.

"I thought if it wasn't safe the Coast Guard wouldn't have passed it and the company wouldn't let it sail," he reasoned.

He had approached Captain Crawley with his concerns. When, he asked, would the rivets be fixed? According to Hale, Crawley couldn't answer that. "We're never in port long enough," Crawley said.

Hale's statements added weight to an issue that was becoming a major focus in the hearings: the structural integrity of the older vessels in Great Lakes shipping. With the loss of the *Bradley* in 1958 and the damage to the *Townsend* in almost the same location as the split in the *Morrell*, questions were raised about whether these long, aging vessels were safe when they were taking a pounding in cold, stormy waters. Perhaps shipping companies should consider retiring the older freighters—those constructed before 1948, when new steel began to be used in the making of hulls, or at least the ones built in the early 1900s—or they should be kept at port when stormy weather was predicted. This placed the responsibility on the shoulders of the shipping companies and the Coast Guard.

James C. Sherman of the U.S. Salvage Association supported the present system. "There are no guidelines in terms of definite time limits on retiring ships," he said. "We feel that it should be based on inspections and the condition of the vessel."

Michigan Congressman John Dingell, a member of the House Merchant Marine and Fisheries Committee, felt a need for new guidelines for retiring older boats like the *Morrell*. "There must be a limit, and I cannot help but wonder whether we are watching the aging of our lakers closely enough," he said. "Many other carriers operating on the lakes are similarly aged and are rapidly becoming obsolete."

Dingell further urged the Coast Guard board to expand its investigation to include reporting on the safety standards of all Great Lakes vessels. Stricter guidelines, he felt, were needed.

The United Steelworkers union, which represented the sailors on the Great Lakes, weighed in with its worries about the safety measures on the carriers. "The present archaic safety requirements give the seaman of the Great Lakes less than a 50–50 chance of survival in the event of a ship disaster," the union's representative pointed out. The union recommended that the present safety and inspection programs be rejected and updated, and that the Coast Guard be given authority to keep boats in port during bad weather. Improvements—an auxiliary power source in the front section of a boat, for instance—had to be made to avoid the kind of catastrophe that occurred with the *Morrell*.

> > >

The board of inquiry adjourned during the holiday season, and efforts to locate the *Morrell* were suspended. After the first of the year, however, finding the wreckage became a prime objective for the Coast Guard. Admiral Willard J. Smith contracted Ocean Systems Inc., an Alexandria, Virginia, firm headed by Jon Lindbergh, son of the famed aviator Charles Lindbergh, to find and survey the *Morrell*'s wreckage. In 1965, Ocean Systems had bolstered its reputation by locating a hydrogen bomb lost off the coast of Spain. The search for the *Morrell* would promise its own challenge. A navy plane, equipped with magnetic anomaly detection equipment,

The *Bramble*, a standard 180-foot Coast Guard cutter, played a vital and extensive role in the *Morrell* story, first in the search for victims and later as the vessel used in the discovery of the boat's wrecked stern section. U.S. Coast Guard photograph.

would fly over the area where the *Morrell* was believed to have gone down, and when a large object was discovered, Ocean Systems would sail to the location and, using a remote-control camera lowered to the wreck site, attempt to make a positive identification. The *Bramble*, one of the Coast Guard cutters assisting in the search for *Morrell* survivors a month earlier, would serve as the survey vessel.

The *Bramble* sailed to a point about twenty miles north-northwest of the Michigan "thumb" and waited for directions from the navy plane. The wait was brief. As recalled by Roland Schultz, a crewman aboard the *Bramble,* the plane reported a hit within fifteen to twenty minutes of the beginning of the search. The object in the water was just over four miles from the *Bramble*'s position.

As Schultz noted, this was only the beginning. Once she had reached the reported position, the *Bramble* spent three days "slowly steaming in squares, rectangles and circles," looking for the sunken object's precise location, which could only be determined by passing directly over the wreck. High-tech side-scan sonar was still something in the future.

The search was rewarded on January 6, thirty-eight days after the *Morrell* was lost. The *Bramble* maneuvered into a position from which the Oceans Systems team could lower a remote-control camera, complete with lighting, from the *Bramble*'s buoy boom. Schultz's account captures the surprise and feeling of accomplishment felt on the Coast Guard cutter:

> Remarkably, within minutes of being deployed over the side, an image of a vertical wall materialized on the black-and-white TV monitor within the *Bramble*'s chart room, which had been configured as a control room. Those of us known as the "bridge gang" had suddenly invented reasons to be present in this small compartment, watching in silent awe as the operator passed the camera about the riveted hull of a ship.

The positive identification came much easier than anyone anticipated. The TV monitor was clearly showing the stern section of a vessel, and when the camera was run from left to right, the lettering on the boat spelling out *Daniel J. Morrell* could be seen, the black water eerily lit by lights mounted on the camera frame.

The next step: send divers down for close-up inspection of the wreck.

Over the next few days, Ocean Systems personnel converted the deck of the *Bramble* into a diving platform. A decompression chamber was

A diver prepares to explore the stern section of the *Morrell*. Photograph by Roland Schultz, QM-1 U.S. Coast Guard.

welded to the deck; other tools of the diving trade, including precautionary safety measures, were secured to the deck as well. The *Morrell*'s stern was in 216 feet of water, which meant that, at a time before the complex mixtures of gases used today, a diver had only about fifteen minutes of bottom time before he had to begin his return to the *Bramble*. The diver would be required to make two stops before reaching the surface, and then he would be taken for a lengthy stay in the decompression chamber.

Exploring the wreckage was only part of the mission. Divers were also to bring up metal samples from the *Morrell*'s hull for analysis by the Battelle Memorial Institute in Columbus, Ohio.

The wreckage of the *Daniel J. Morrell* spoke in great detail of the freighter's violent end. By all indications, the stern section had plunged, forward first, almost vertically to the bottom of Lake Huron, scooping up a large

The engine room, now silent, ran the stern portion of the *Morrell* long after the bow portion sank. Photograph by John Janzen.

The auxiliary wheel crusted with mussels. Photograph by John Janzen.

volume of mud as she gouged the lake's floor before coming to rest, upright and listing slightly to port; the wreckage was buried in mud to within six feet of her deck. The break, between the eleventh and twelfth hatches, confirmed Hale's story about the location of the split. The twisting and tearing of steel at the breaking point were extraordinary. The steel was torn, folded, and jagged. The cargo hatch covers were strewn about. The covered starboard lifeboat hung over the side of the boat, untouched by anyone attempting to abandon ship; the port lifeboat was missing. No victims could be found, nor was the bow portion of the *Morrell* anywhere in the area. A clock onboard indicated that the stern had slipped beneath the surface at 3:28 a.m. If Hale had been accurate in his estimation of the time of the bow's sinking, the stern had continued to sail for nearly an hour and a half after the bow's sinking.

Divers visited the wreck every day, weather permitting, until February 2. They used handheld cameras to videotape as much of the wreckage as possible, but poor weather conditions and stirred-up silt reduced visibility. A camera and lights mounted on a frame offered much more success. The metal samples were collected and sent up to the *Bramble*.

❯ ❯ ❯

The Coast Guard board released its final report on March 24, 1967, nearly five months after the loss of the *Daniel J. Morrell*. A thorough representation of the different voices heard by the board, the report provided a description of the vessel and an account of her final trip, as reported by Hale. The *Morrell*'s repair and recent inspection history were included, as were the differing views of the condition of the boat at the time of her sinking. Weather conditions were recorded. The report outlined the search for the wreckage and offered a detailed description of the condition of the sunken stern section. The narrative, given in flat declarative sentences, might not have made for scintillating reading, but it served its purpose. The board carefully avoided offering opinion or interpretation. After months of sitting in rooms full of lawyers and reporters, the board knew better than to provide them with anything that could be used in lawsuit proceedings. Their written recommendations, however, left little doubt about what bothered the board members about this particular accident.

Although it was impossible to rule conclusively that metal fatigue and brittle steel caused by cold air and water temperatures were the sole reasons for the loss of the *Morrell*, the Coast Guard Board of Inquiry declared that these probably were a contributing factor, if not *the* contributing factor leading to the boat's breaking apart. The study of the samples taken from the sunken vessel indicated a weakening of the steel common in boats built prior to 1948. The Coast Guard weighed other factors when coming to their ruling regarding the structural failure of the *Morrell*:

> The Board finds the cause of this accident with attendant loss of life was the structural failure of the main hull girder amidships, which caused the vessel to break in two and both sections to sink. Factors which are considered to have contributed to this structural failure are: high longitudinal stress on the hull girder due to height and wave length of the seas; limited original design section modulus for a vessel having such a large length to depth ratio; use in the original construction of the vessel of steel which is highly notch sensitive at the low atmospheric and sea temperatures experienced; a notch in the structure which was the nucleus of the initial fracture; low cycle stress fatigue; and steel of high transition temperature characteristics, relatively susceptible to brittle fracture.

The general alarm, last used to alert the crew that the *Morrell* was sinking, as photographed by divers exploring the wreckage. Photograph by John Janzen.

The report went on to recommend thorough inspections of all older vessels' hulls and, if deemed necessary, the fortification of hulls judged to be weakening from age. The board absolved Captain Arthur Crawley of any blame for the loss of the *Morrell*, finding that it would not have been possible for Crawley to know of weaknesses in his boat's hull; he could rely only on the boat's recent inspections when considering his vessel's strength against a storm on the lakes.

Some of the report's recommendations addressed safety issues that had been examined—and largely ignored—in the past. The hearings had noted the slim chances of a sailor's survival if tossed into the frigid water during a November storm, and captains of boats out on Lake Huron during the *Morrell* storm unanimously agreed that there was no way a lifeboat could have been launched in such weather conditions. Hale had delivered moving testimony about his and his crewmates' fight for survival on the raft, further illustrating what the board of inquiry already knew: even if crew members reached a life raft and were physically removed from the water, they were still in grave danger of hypothermia before help arrived. In this regard, the board recommended that commercial shipping vessels be equipped with inflatable, capsule-style life rafts. These rafts enclosed the crew members and sheltered them from the elements, and would have flare guns, a radio, and other equipment giving those onboard a significantly better chance of survival than the barrel-type of raft currently used.

In drawing its conclusions and making its recommendations, the Coast Guard board was nothing if not thorough. The board members were rightfully concerned about how the lack of communication might have affected rescue attempts. The boat's loss of power prohibited an SOS transmission—or communication with the stern of the boat, for that matter. No one knew the *Morrell* was in distress. To make matters worse, nearly a day and a half passed before Bethlehem Steel alerted the Coast Guard about its concerns about the welfare of the *Daniel J. Morrell*. By then, hope of finding survivors had all but vanished. There was really no excuse for either of these problems.

The board made a point of absolving the *Morrell*'s owners of blame in these communications issues. "The radio installation on the DANIEL J. MORRELL met the requirements of the applicable Federal Regulations," the report states. "The system proved to be inadequate under the existing circumstances." Emergency radios, the report goes on, were not required

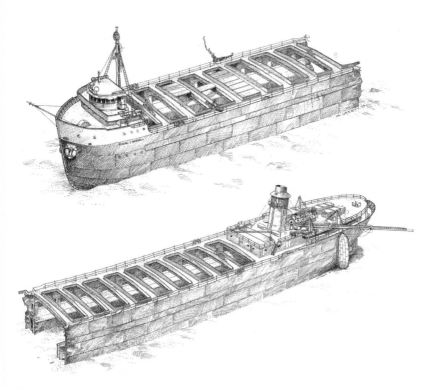

The stern portion of the *Morrell* stayed afloat and under power for an hour and a half after the sinking of the bow. Illustrations by Robert McGreevy; courtesy of the artist.

on Great Lakes freighters. In the wake of this most recent tragedy, it was time to make changes.

The board recommended a change in federal regulations. An emergency power source should be required on the forward section of every Great Lakes vessel. In addition, the board felt that the Federal Communications Commission should be urged to require "an emergency radio with a self-contained source of power" on all commercial vessels. Neither of these suggestions would be difficult to implement.

"More lives might have been saved if a distress signal had been transmitted," the board concluded. These two recommendations would see that a pilothouse would be capable of sending an SOS under circumstances like the *Morrell*'s.

The five members of the board of inquiry pushed for better communications between shipping company officials and their boats out on the lakes, suggesting that there be contact on a regularly scheduled basis, at least once every twenty-four hours. The *Morrell*, of course, was already operating under this reporting system. The Coast Guard went a step further in its recommendations: if a company hadn't heard from a vessel within an hour of the reporting time, the owner would then initiate a search for the boat's whereabouts; there would be no more assumptions about the safety of a vessel. This recommendation had very little teeth in terms of saving survivors, and it would have been of no use in the case of the *Morrell*, which had sunk in an unknown location. The board did make one recommendation that would have alerted the Coast Guard of the sinking *and* would have provided the exact location of the wreckage: a datum marker buoy that would be activated before a ship sank or, at the very least, be activated automatically when a vessel sank to a predetermined depth. "This could be stowed with one of the required liferafts or attached with a pressure-release device to the side of the pilothouse," the report proposed.

The report ultimately proved a point made by shipwreck historians everywhere: with very few exceptions, shipwrecks are caused by more than one factor, and these factors usually combine human error or misunderstanding with factors out of human control, or factors that humans chose to ignore. In this case, you had an aging boat with a weakened hull, a brutal storm, and a captain's decision to sail; remove any of those factors and the *Morrell* would have reached her destination.

Dennis Hale poses at his Rock Creek, Ohio, home in 2006 with the life jacket he was wearing at the time of the *Morrell*'s sinking. Aside from the life jacket, he was wearing only a peacoat and boxer shorts. Photograph by *Chicago Tribune*/Getty Images.

AFTERWORD

O N APRIL 1, 1967, THE DEPARTMENT OF TRANSPORTATION
assigned the newly created National Transportation Safety Board
(NTSB) the responsibility of determining the cause of shipping accidents
such as the *Daniel J. Morrell*. Since the Coast Guard Board of Inquiry had
completed its study of the *Morrell* only days earlier, on March 21, it made
little sense for the NTSB to conduct its own hearings. Still, after carefully
examining the Coast Guard board's report, as well as actions taken as a
result of the report, the NSTB offered recommendations and observations
of its own.

The NTSB did not dispute the board of inquiry's findings on the cause
of the *Morrell's* sinking, nor did it disagree with the board's recommendations concerning communications and safety improvements. However,
the NTSB was not satisfied with the initial response to the Coast Guard
board's recommendations regarding the strengthening of hulls built prior
to 1948, and in a February 8, 1968, letter to Admiral Willard Smith, NTSB
chairman Joseph O'Connell worried that "a similar tragedy may occur to
other bulk carriers under similar circumstances," that the NSTB was "also
concerned with measures to prevent the failure of the hull girder in vessels
[similar to the *Morrell*, *Carl D. Bradley*, and *Edward Y. Townsend*]."

O'Connell proposed two specific solutions to the issue:

1. "Strengthen the deck and/or sheer strake structure in the midships
   area in vessels over 400 feet long constructed prior to 1948, or curtail the operation of these vessels during specific days and period of
   the fall season when adverse weather and wave conditions approach
   or exceed those encountered by the SS Daniel J. Morrell"; and
2. "Based on the special inspection program, implement a progressive
   structural renewal program on an individual ship basis."

While not a formal rebuke of the Coast Guard's actions following the release of the board of inquiry's report, the letter made clear that more had to be done to satisfy the NTSB. In an earlier letter from Smith to O'Connell, dated October 4, 1967, Smith had listed some of the measures taken by the Coast Guard since the *Morrell* tragedy. The Coast Guard had acted on its report's recommendations. Sixteen vessels had been tested for structural integrity, and two were judged to be in need of "corrective action." One had been repaired, and the other removed from service until repairs were made. Other studies, including on wave action, stress measuring and recording, and the strength of newer 700-foot vessels and projected 1,000-footers, were being conducted.

The biggest enemy, as always, was time. It took months or years to make some decisions and change protocol. With other accidents to older vessels possible—Admiral Smith wrote that that the average age of Great Lakes bulk carriers was forty-five years, and that boats constructed in the fifty- to sixty-year range constituted more vessels than in any other ten-year period—time was the enemy of safety.

A case in point: In March 1969, the Coast Guard announced a new policy for merchant vessel reporting. Under the new policy, if a boat was more than four hours late in reporting, a "communication search" was to begin. If contact with the missing boat was not made, planes and boats were to be dispatched to look for the missing vessel.

More than two years had passed since the lack of communication had been a factor in the loss of life onboard the *Daniel J. Morrell*.

> > >

The *Edward Y. Townsend* spent the better part of two years tied up at the Algoma Central Railway dock in Sault Ste. Marie, her certificate of inspection pulled by the Coast Guard since December 2, 1966, her owners and operators weighing the advantages of putting her back in service against the costs of repairing her and making her seaworthy again. At her age, the *Townsend* was well past her prime: Gigantic 700-foot-plus freighters such as the *Edmund Fitzgerald*, *Arthur B. Homer*, and *Edward L. Ryerson* were hauling cargo tonnage, at greater speed, which the older boats could not begin to match.

Bethlehem Steel officials ultimately decided that the *Townsend* was more valuable as scrap than the costs of placing her back in service. A

The *Townsend* was eventually sold for scrap. In this photograph she is being towed by the tug *Salvage Monarch*, bound for Spain in September 1968. She broke in two and sank in a storm near Newfoundland. Photograph by Tom Manse. Courtesy of Roger LeLievre, Great Lakes and Seaway Shipping On-Line, Inc.

salvage company in Spain wanted the *Townsend*, supposedly to cut down for reuse in shipbuilding.

On September 13, 1968, the *Townsend* began her final voyage. With two tugboats towing her, the *Townsend* took one last look at the Great Lakes, beginning with Lake Superior, then moving south and east, down Lake Huron and across Lakes Erie and Ontario, missing only Lake Michigan in her tour of some of the largest bodies of fresh water in the world. An uneventful trip up the St. Lawrence Seaway brought her to the Atlantic Ocean. It was a journey taken by countless foreign vessels over the decades, vessels that crossed the Atlantic before bringing or taking home package freight. The long route created some anxious moments when a European ship running behind schedule had to hurry to reach the St. Lawrence before it closed for winter.

The *Townsend* had no such concerns when the *Hudson*, a Dutch tug hired to tow the *Townsend* and *Dolomite*, a Canadian freighter, left to cross the Atlantic. On October 7 the three vessels ran into a heavy storm about four hundred miles southeast of St. John's, Newfoundland. The unmanned *Townsend* broke free from the tug and, tossed about in the storm, broke apart, sinking to the depths of the ocean, her end eerily similar to the fate of her sister ship.

> > >

After years of legal discussions and maneuvering, the lawsuits against Bethlehem Steel were resolved. The focus of the suits had been safety, with the families of the lost sailors claiming that the *Daniel J. Morrell* had been structurally unsafe to sail, and Bethlehem Steel contesting the claim. Bethlehem Steel did not contest the Coast Guard's Board of Inquiry ruling, seconded by the National Transportation Safety Board, that the cause of the *Morrell*'s loss had been structural failure; the fact that she had split apart made that obvious. The big question centered on the steel company's culpability: if the Coast Guard exonerated Captain Crawley for his decision to sail on grounds that he could not have possibly known that the freighter's hull had been weakened by years of work in stormy weather, and concluded that the boat had sunk as a result of a weakened hull tested by heavy seas, how could one hold the company responsible for trusting its vessel's master and the Coast Guard inspection conclusions?

The case was hindered further by the lack of a crucial piece of evidence: the bow section had yet to be located. The Battelle Memorial Institute of Columbus Laboratories had studied samples taken from the stern portion of the boat and concluded that the steel used in its construction would become brittle under the conditions the *Morrell* encountered, so there was no doubt about what would be found regarding the metal on the bow section. Still, attorneys would have preferred to have a survey of the complete wreckage before a final decision was reached.

The real issue, of course, was money. Twenty-eight families of deceased sailors, plus Dennis Hale as the lone survivor, were entitled compensation. In the weeks following the loss of the *Morrell*, lawsuits filed by the individual families began to pile up until, on January 24, 1967, a Cleveland judge ordered a halt to the suits until the liability of the *Morrell*'s owners was determined. At that point, the families' lawsuits totaled nearly ten million dollars overall, while Bethlehem Steel sought a $400,000 limit for all claims.

Other suits were filed in Buffalo, with perhaps the most interesting being filed by Cecelia Ann Stojek, whose husband, Art, had died on the raft. Mrs. Stojek asked for $500,000 for the loss of her husband's earnings, and an additional $250,000 for the pain and suffering he had endured on the raft.

In his initial suit, filed on December 8, a week after he was rescued from the raft, Dennis Hale asked for $150,000, but he amended that figure to $500,000 a year later. The *Morrell*, he claimed in his suit, was unseaworthy, and her operators had failed to repair the boat and provide adequate emergency equipment. As a result of the sinking, he suffered excruciating pain that caused hallucinations and a wish for death, and permanently disabled him from working as a seaman.

After more than four years, Bethlehem Steel finally settled with the heirs of the deceased sailors on December 9, 1970. The company agreed to pay $2.75 million—the largest settlement in maritime history—to be divided among the families of the lost sailors. The distribution of the settlement money was based on the size of the sailor's family—the more children, the more money.

Hale, in a separate agreement, reached what he called a "fair settlement." As part of the agreement, he was not permitted to reveal how much money he received.

❯ ❯ ❯

Spring 1979. Nearly thirteen years had passed since the *Daniel J. Morrell* had been lost in the November storm. The bow section of the wreckage had yet to be discovered. The *Edmund Fitzgerald*, the largest and in 1975 the most recent vessel to be lost in the Great Lakes, its two gigantic pieces submerged in more than five hundred feet of Lake Superior water, had become the shipwreck explorers' prize. The *Morrell* seemed to have sailed away into history.

Shipwreck hunter David Trotter, a former executive at Ford Motors, had located wrecks on each of the Great Lakes but Lake Ontario, and he had explored more of Lake Huron than anyone in the business. By today's standards, the equipment he used for locating and diving wrecks in those days was primitive. Finding a wreck required a certain amount of luck.

Locating the *Morrell*, in Trotter's view, took much more than just a touch of good fortune.

"When you think of the odds, it's sort of like divine intervention," he said, more than thirty-five years after the discovery of the bow section.

In 1977, Trotter became the second on Lake Huron to own a long-range navigation system (LRN-C), which could be used to approximate location. After getting the LRN-C numbers for the Port Austin Reef Lighthouse, he tried to calculate the location of the *Morrell*'s stern section. He and his team sailed to the calculated area and, using a side-scan sonar, searched for a large object on the lake floor. As they had hoped, they found something, in roughly two hundred feet of water.

The dive to the object was riskier than it would be today. In 1979, they were still using regular air, rather than mixed gases, to dive deeper wrecks. Diver's narcosis affected everyone and strictly limited a diver's time on the bottom. Often compared to the effects one encounters after heavy drinking, diver's narcosis could have a strong effect on a diver's mood, motor functions, and judgment. Divers used what they termed the "Martini Law" to measure the effects of the narcosis at any given depth of a dive: the narcosis was not an issue in a dive under sixty-six feet, but every descent of thirty-three feet thereafter had the effect of drinking one martini. Shipwreck explorers, of course, were aware of what could happen, and they used extreme caution in how deep and how long they would dive. Trotter admitted that his crew was "narc'd" when they dove the *Morrell*, but they were experienced enough to deal with it.

Dana Engel and Larry Copland, Trotter's associates, dove the wreck first and confirmed that it was, indeed, the stern of the *Daniel J. Morrell*. This, however, was only the beginning. It was still early enough in the day that they decided to move out farther in the lake and see what they might find. According to Trotter, there was no firm plan, no great expectation; they were going to see what they could turn up, if anything. They just figured to sail about five miles or so, drop the side-scan sonar, and look for a return.

"Within forty-five minutes, we had another target," Trotter said, still amazed at their good fortune.

Finding the object was a mixed blessing: they knew they had found something on the bottom of Lake Huron—and an educated guess would have been the *Morrell*, since nothing else was known to have sunk in that location—but they had to essentially "rediscover" it on another occasion. The LRN-C could approximate location—"you could not be exact"—but you did not have to be off by much to find yourself sailing around on a huge body of water, looking for the proverbial needle in a haystack.

Good fortune was with them again when they set out to find the object three weeks later. Trotter and Copland were returning from the previous expedition, with John Dulzo as the third. They located the sunken object, and Copland was the first to dive. In the murky darkness, he had the feeling of elation that one experiences when encountering a boat that massive

The *Morrell's* bow section was not discovered until May 1979. The boat's clock had stopped at 1:55 a.m., approximately the same time as Dennis Hale had estimated the sinking of the vessel. Photograph by Jack Papes.

on the lake floor. He worked his way up the boat, unsure if he was heading forward or aft, until he saw the red paint on the deck.

"I think we have found the other half of the *Morrell*," he announced after going through the time-consuming decompression necessary for return to the surface. He had not been able to make a positive identification during his brief stay on the bottom; that would be up to one of the other two.

Dulzo was able to do that during his dive. As he swam alongside the sunken freighter, he saw something white in the distance, and the closer he came to it, the more he realized that he was near the front and that the white-painted object was the boat's pilothouse. From there, he made the positive identification. He tied a line to the *Morrell* and returned to the surface.

Trotter's job was to take as many photographs of their discovery as time would permit.

The wreckage, in every sense of the word, was awesome. The bow, like the stern, had come to rest in an upright position. The Cambria logo sat almost regally atop the foremast, and the *Morrell* anchors were still in place. The boat's violent end was as evident as the damage in the stern, from the

A diver hovers over the *Morrell*'s pilothouse, once the site of great activity aboard the giant ore carrier. Photograph by Jack Papes.

Sitting upright two hundred feet below the surface of Lake Huron, the bow of the *Morrell* rises like a ghostly presence on the lake's floor. Photograph by Jack Papes.

Divers examine one of the unused lifeboats resting on the floor of Lake Huron. Photograph by Jack Papes.

tremendous rending of steel from the *Morrell's* tearing apart to the hatch covers blown out during her drop to the bottom of the lake. What Trotter's photography—or anyone else's in the future, for that matter—could not capture was the sheer size of the wreck.

Inside the pilothouse, a clock froze at 1:55 a.m., charting the bow's time of death and verifying the fact that the stern had sailed slightly more than an hour and a half before giving in to nature's wishes. This meant that the men on the stern section had more than enough time to consider their fates after the sinking of the bow. Their only hope would have been for a freighter in the area to see them. One could only imagine their horror as they came up from below decks and saw what was left of the *Morrell* and witnessed how the massive cargo hold was filling with water. No one would ever know how many had gathered on the stern's life raft, similar to the way the officers and crewmen had taken positions on the forward raft, only to be hurled into the icy water. All but one of the crew from the stern had been recovered; all of the victims had drowned or died of hypothermia.

The wreckage of the bow represented the terrible beauty of a shipwreck: for all its majesty and history, it ultimately stood as a mute witness to unspeakable loss.

> > >

Dennis Hale never sailed again. In the years immediately following the loss of the *Daniel J. Morrell*, he struggled with post-traumatic stress issues and strong feelings of survivor's guilt, his life a series of highs and lows largely based on his connection to the *Daniel J. Morrell*.

"I don't want to be Dennis Hale, the only survivor of a shipwreck," he would complain. "I just want to be Dennis Hale."

The two survivors of the wreck of the *Carl D. Bradley* had similar problems. They were largely shunned by the townspeople in Rogers City, Michigan, where they resided and where the great majority of the lost sailors' families lived. In such a small town, the bitterness was oppressive. Elmer Fleming, the *Bradley*'s first mate, agonized over his lost crewmates, and the trauma of the sinking was such that when he returned to sailing and was awarded a skipper's position on his own boat, he was unable to handle rough weather and had to resign his position. He spent the rest of his days wondering why he had survived and the others had not.

Frank Mays, on the other hand, never returned to the lakes. He, too, found that only a few friends would drop by and visit him at home after his release from the hospital, and, like Fleming, he became a virtual persona non grata in his own hometown. "Had I done something wrong by surviving?" he asked himself.

Hale had other problems. He had not come from a small city that lost twenty-two of its citizens and another five from towns nearby, where the loss to the community was so palpable. Only two of the *Morrell* victims—Arthur Fargo and Hale's friend Saverio Grippi—hailed from Hale's hometown of Ashtabula. But Hale had a hint of what the two *Bradley* survivors had to deal with when he visited Grippi's wife shortly after his return to Ashtabula; it had gone poorly and Grippi's sister-in-law, at the house when Hale visited, told Hale that it might be better if he did not come back.

He internalized much of what haunted him. After the initial onslaught of media interest, he spoke sparingly about the *Morrell*, and he tried to change the subject whenever it came up in conversation with coworkers. He felt that he had lost his privacy, that he was recognized and stared at when he went out in public. He drank, smoked marijuana, and took other controlled substances to deaden his pain. He ran around with other women, and his marriage ended—as did the one after that. He was terrified of storms to such an extent that he would take his family into the basement whenever the weather grew nasty. Being the survivor, he admitted, made him feel "dirty, unclean, and ashamed."

Part of his mental anguish could be attributed to his physical misery, which served as a constant reminder of the *Morrell* and his ordeal on the raft. The recovery process exacted its own psychological toll. After Hale's rescue and admission to the hospital in Harbor Beach, the emphasis had been on the immediate: elevate the body temperature, treat the frostbite to fight off gangrene, check for circulatory or nerve damage. Other physical and psychological rehabilitation would have to wait. Hale was urged to stay patient.

When he was transferred to the hospital in Ashtabula, he still had no feeling in his feet and parts of his legs. He began to move about with a walker shortly after his return home, but it was very uncomfortable. He developed hammertoes, which made walking even more difficult. Calcified from a lack of use, his big toe on his right foot was almost immobile. He lost some of the feeling and movement in his left hand.

The recovery would take years, and even then he would never regain full strength in his feet. The little toe and a small portion of his left foot were eventually amputated. He had ten operations on his left foot alone. As he wrote in his autobiography, he would always be reminded of the *Morrell*. "I guess you could say that every step that I take is a reminder of the night of the sinking and the friends I lost."

Hale never went back to working on the lakes, but the boats and his friends were never far from his mind. During the 1970s, he acted as an advocate for safety in the shipping industry, with only minimal success. He petitioned the highest sources, going so far as to write President Jimmy Carter in the White House, but his letters were often ignored, and in some cases he was patronized by recipients. He was hit hard by the loss of the *Edmund Fitzgerald*.

In 1981, Hale was invited to attend and, if he wished, speak at Lake Superior State College in Sault Ste. Marie. Larry Coplin had filmed a documentary about the *Morrell* and would be presenting it at the college. Hale was to be the guest of honor.

Hale told the organizers that he would attend, but he had no interest in speaking at the event. He had not talked publicly about the *Morrell* shipwreck since he had given his accounts in interviews in the weeks following the accident. Fifteen years had passed, and he could not imagine a circumstance where he would feel comfortable reliving his experiences in public.

He certainly didn't want to answer questions about events that were still painful for him to remember.

He changed his mind when he traveled to Sault Ste. Marie and saw the college's displays of shipwreck memorabilia and learned that the banquet was being dedicated to the crew of the *Daniel J. Morrell*. He would speak, after all. Frightened that he might freeze up in front of an audience, he jotted down some notes on index cards.

The event turned out to be cathartic. His reservations dissipated as soon as he started speaking at the podium at the front of the packed hall. He had worried about what he would say, but once he began, words long bottled up within him came flooding out.

"I started somewhat hesitantly," he remembered, "but upon seeing how moved the audience was by hearing my tale, I continued with more confidence."

He wept occasionally while telling his story. As difficult as it was, he gained a sense of liberation from offering his account to these total strangers. He said nothing of his visions on the raft—"I was unsure how the audience would respond"—but he told the rest. "When I finished," he said, "I felt as if a great weight had been lifted from my shoulders."

For Hale, narrating his account to others amounted to more than freeing himself from the captivity of his past; it was also a way of honoring his dead crewmates and keeping their memories alive. Programs similar to the one at Lake Superior State College would pop up in the future, and Hale told his story more frequently and with less stress as each year passed. He attended Great Lakes maritime conventions and memorials for the *Carl D. Bradley* and *Edmund Fitzgerald*. He granted interviews to newspapers and magazines and appeared in a cable television documentary being filmed about the *Fitzgerald*. He dictated his story to Tim Juhl, Pat Stayer, and Jim Stayer; the book, *Sole Survivor*, was published by Out of the Blue Productions in 1996. *Shipwrecked*, a much longer, self-published account that includes stories about his childhood, hit bookstore shelves in 2010.

He also conquered his fear of going out on the water. In 1999, thirty-three years after his final trip on the *Morrell*, he was invited to spend six days on the *Roger Blough*, an 835-foot bulk carrier. To ease his apprehension about sailing again, Hale was told that he could bring seven friends with him.

The group boarded the *Blough* in Sault Ste. Marie. The boat was bound for Two Harbors, Minnesota, for a load of taconite; from there, it was on

The wrecked bow and stern sections of the *Morrell* now rest quietly on the floor of Lake Huron. Illustrations by Robert McGreevy. Kenneth Thro Collection, University of Wisconsin–Superior.

Dennis Hale held a rope connected to the wreckage of the *Daniel J. Morrell*. He hoped that people might be inspired by the tales of his survival. Photograph by Skip Kadar. Courtesy of Gary Venet, Rec & Tec Dive Charters, Inc.

to Chicago. Hale spent time in the pilothouse and engine room, chatting with those on duty and learning everything he could about the *Blough*. Rather than being overwhelmed by sailing on a gigantic ore carrier for the first time since the *Morrell*, Hale was reminded of the camaraderie—the sense of family—that he had enjoyed when he worked on the boats. "It felt like I was putting on a pair of old shoes," he said.

This, along with a few other excursions on much smaller vessels, prepared Hale for a trip that would bring closure to his *Morrell* experiences. In 2009, the Yap Filming Company contacted Hale about appearing in a six-part cable documentary series it was producing on the sinking of the *Edmund Fitzgerald*. Would he be willing to talk about his experiences for the series? If so, a filming crew and divers would be visiting the site of the *Daniel J. Morrell's* wrecked bow section. Hale agreed without hesitation.

On June 10, Hale boarded the dive boat, along with Gary Venet, the boat's captain; Victor Kushmaniuk, the documentary's director; and the boat's crew and divers. The trip to the *Morrell's* site took two hours. The weather was nearly perfect, and Lake Huron was calm. On the way out, Hale talked on camera about his survival. Later, one of the divers, after his dive to the *Morrell*'s bow had been completed, would marvel at Hale's survival. "I'm so cold I can hardly stand it," he admitted, noting that the water temperature of the lake was not much colder than the water temperature on the water that night in 1966.

The dive to the wreck took the better of two hours, including decompression time, and while those onboard the boat waited for the divers to return with their report, Hale talked more for the cameras. This was as close as he had been to the *Morrell* since he watched the bow disappear beneath the stormy waters forty-three years earlier, and while he was trying to hold up in front of the cameras, he felt a surge of powerful emotions. A plastic line connected the dive boat to the wreckage, and at one point, someone handed Hale the line. Everyone nearby moved away, leaving Hale alone with his thoughts.

CREW OF THE *DANIEL J. MORRELL*

NOVEMBER 29, 1966

Bragg, Norman M., 40, Niagara Falls, New York, Watchman

Campbell, Stuart A., 60, Marinette, Wisconsin, Wheelsman

Cleary, John J., Jr., 20, Cleveland, Ohio, Deckhand

Crawley, Arthur I., 47, Rocky River, Ohio, Master

Dahl, George A., 38, Duluth, Minnesota, Third Assistant Engineer

Davis, Larry G., 27, Toledo, Ohio, Deckwatch

Fargo, Arthur S., 52, Ashtabula, Ohio, Fireman

Fosbender, Charles M., 42, St. Clair, Michigan, Wheelsman

Grippi, Saverio, 53, Ashtabula, Ohio, Coal Passer

Groh, John M., 21, Erie, Pennsylvania, Deckwatch

Hale, Dennis, 26, Ashtabula, Ohio, Deckwatch

Homick, Nicholas P., 35, Hudson, Pennsylvania, Second Cook

Kapets, Phillip E., 51, Ironwood, Michigan, First Mate

Konieczka, Chester, 45, Hamburg, New York, Fireman

MacLeod, Duncan R., 61, Gloucester, Massachusetts, Second Mate

Mahsem, Joseph A., 59, Duluth, Minnesota, Porter

Marchildon, Valmour A., 43, Kenmore, New York, First Assistant Engineer

Marcotte, Ernest G., 62, Waterford, Michigan, Third Mate

Norkunas, Alfred G., 39, Superior, Wisconsin, Second Assistant Engineer

Price, David L., 19, Cleveland, Ohio, Coal Passer

Rischmiller, Henry, 34, Williamsville, New York, Wheelsman

Satlawa, Stanley J., 39, Buffalo, New York, Steward (missing)

Schmidt, John H., 46, Toledo, Ohio, Chief Engineer

Sestakauskas, Charles J., 49, Buffalo, New York, Porter

Simpson, Wilson E., 50, Albemarle, North Carolina, Oiler

Stojek, Arthur E., 41, Buffalo, New York, Deckhand

Truman, Leon R., 45, Toledo, Ohio, Coal Passer

Whoeme, Albert P., 51, Knife River, Minnesota, Watchman

Worcester, Donald E., 38, Columbia Falls, Maine, Oiler

GLOSSARY

aft (or after deck). Back, or stern, of a ship or boat.

ballast. Added weight, usually lake water, to lower the ship in the water and add stability.

ballast tanks. Large, watertight storage tanks below the cargo hold, on the starboard and port sides of the ship, where ballast is stored.

barge. A vessel, usually without power, that carries cargo and is towed by another vessel.

beam. The breadth of a ship at its widest point.

boat. Great Lakes vessels are usually referred to as "boats"; ocean-going vessels are referred to as "ships."

bow. Front, or forward section, of a ship or boat.

bulkhead. Partition used to divide sections of the hull.

buoy. A cautionary marker warning boats of shallow water, objects in the water, and other problems or dangers.

capsize. To roll onto a side or turn over.

captain (or master). Commander, or chief officer, of a boat or ship.

chief engineer. Crewman in charge of a boat's engine.

de-ballasting. The process of pumping, or expelling, water from a ship's ballast tanks.

deck. The flat surface of a vessel.

deckwatch. Crew assigned to watch for other boats, buoys, or hazards on the water.

draft. Depth of a ship's hull beneath the waterline.

first mate. The second in command of a boat or ship.

fitting out. The process of preparing a ship for sailing after construction or layup.

flotsam. Floating wreckage or debris.

fore (or foredeck). Forward, or bow, section of a boat or ship.

founder. To fill with water and sink.

freeboard. Distance between the waterline and the spar deck.

galley. A vessel's kitchen.

green water. Solid water, rather than spray, washing over the decks of a vessel.

grounding. Striking bottom, or running completely aground.

hatch covers. Large sheets of steel that cover the hatch coamings and prevent water from entering the cargo hold.

hatches. Openings in the ship's spar deck through which cargo is loaded and unloaded.

hogging. The bending down of the front and back of a freighter, with no support for the middle.

hold. The large area of a ship in which cargo is stored.

hull. Main body of a boat or ship, on which the decks and superstructures are built.

keel. Backbone of the vessel, running the entire length of a ship, on which the framework of the ship is built.

lee. The protected side of a vessel, away from the direction of the wind.

light. A vessel is traveling "light" if not carrying cargo.

list. A boat's leaning or tipping to one side.

pilothouse (or wheelhouse). Enclosed deck where the wheel and map room are located; the uppermost deck on a vessel.

port. Left side of a ship when one is facing the bow.

porter. A steward's assistant.

screw. The boat's propeller.

Soo. Common term for the locks at Sault Ste. Marie, Michigan.

spar deck (or weather deck). Deck where the hatches are located.

starboard. Right side of a ship when one is facing the bow.

stern. Back, or after section, of a ship or boat.

steward. A vessel's cook.

superstructure. Structures and cabins built above the hull of a ship.

wheelsman. Crew member who steers a vessel.

working. A vessel's twisting, springing, and flexing in heavy seas.

MARINE BOARD OF INVESTIGATION REPORT

A LTHOUGH DESIGNED TO DETERMINE THE CIRCUMSTANCES surrounding the sinking of a vessel, and suggest what measures, if any, might be taken to prevent a similar loss in the future, Coast Guard accident reports bore the heavy weight of legal action. Any shipwreck resulting in the loss of human life cried out for the assignment of blame. Had the boat been properly designed, constructed, and maintained? Was human error, mainly on the part of the vessel's master, largely responsible for the sinking? Were unreasonable demands on the part of the owners and operators components in the decision to sail in hazardous conditions? Was it a matter of the forces of nature overwhelming a boat caught out in an unpredictably vicious storm? Was the boat properly equipped with lifesaving devices that might have been deployed when and after the vessel sank? Was any kind of negligence involved? The answers to these and other questions not only led to *what* the Coast Guard Board of Inquiry would conclude in their findings of the factors leading to the loss of a vessel; they also led to *how* the board worded its final report.

This is important to bear in mind when reading one of the Coast Guard's accident reports. A poorly worded declarative sentence would wind up becoming a focal point in an eventual lawsuit. A badly drawn conclusion could do the same. As a result, Coast Guard officials assigned some of their very best available personnel to conduct the investigation and write the report. The members of a board of inquiry were expected to be knowledgeable enough of the shipping industry to ask the proper questions of those testifying; they were expected to wade through conflicting testimony. Attorneys attending the hearings filled their legal pads with notes. Even if lawsuits weren't filed, there was always the matter of compensation to the families of the lost sailors.

The following Coast Guard report on the loss of the *Daniel J. Morrell* is a strong representation of this sad but important function. It is thorough and objective, cautious in its construction and writing, and firm yet fair in its conclusions. The hearings were conducted almost immediately after the *Morrell*'s sinking, when emotions were running high, attorneys' pencils were being sharpened, and the wreckage had yet to be discovered. (The stern section, as noted in the report, was found while the hearings were in session.) The ferocity of the storm is recalled by those out on Lake Huron as it gathered strength; Thomas Connelly's testimony confirms the struggle the *Morrell* experienced. The narrative of Dennis Hale's remarkable survival is detailed, as is the frantic search for survivors once the fears for the *Morrell* became evident. The Coast Guard officials examine the history of the *Morrell*'s inspections and address the questions of how the communications system was disabled when the boat broke apart, and why so much time passed before anyone felt concern about the *Morrell*'s not contacting its home office. The Coast Guard's recommendations conclude what is a very revealing document.

NATIONAL TRANSPORTATION SAFETY BOARD

Department of Transportation

MARINE ACCIDENT REPORT

Adopted: February 9, 1968   Released: March 4, 1968

——————————o——————————

SINKING OF THE SS DANIEL J. MORRELL
IN LAKE HURON WITH LOSS OF LIFE

November 29, 1966

ACTION BY THE NATIONAL TRANSPORTATION SAFETY BOARD

This marine accident was investigated by the U. S. Coast Guard at a public proceeding in Cleveland, Ohio, conducted December 5, 1966 through March 21, 1967, under authority of 46 USC 239 and the regulations prescribed in 46 CFR 136. The report of this Marine Board of Investigation and the Commandant's action thereon is included in and made a part of this report, for the convenience of the public. By publication of this report, the National Transportation Safety Board does not adopt the portions of the Coast Guard report which are concerned with activities within the exclusive jurisdiction of the Department of Transportation and the U. S. Coast Guard.

The Department of Transportation Act, effective April 1, 1967, assigned the responsibility to the National Transportation Safety Board for determining the cause of transportation accidents, and reporting the facts, conditions, and circumstances related to such accidents. Accordingly, the Board has considered those facts in the Coast Guard report of this accident investigation pertinent to its statutory responsibility to make a determination of the cause.

The Board finds the cause of this accident with attendant loss of life was the structural failure of the main hull girder amidships, which caused the vessel to break in two and both sections to sink. Factors which are considered to have contributed to this structural failure are: high longitudinal stress on the hull girder due to height and wave length of the seas; limited original design section modulus for a vessel having such a large length to depth ratio; use in the original construction of the vessel of steel which is highly notch sensitive at the low atmospheric and sea temperatures experienced; a notch in the structure which was the nucleus of the initial fracture; low cycle stress fatigue; and steel of high transition temperature characteristics, relatively susceptible to brittle fracture.

Factors which are considered to have contributed to loss of life of all but one crew member are (1) no distress signal or communications from the sinking vessel were received, (2) report of the vessel being overdue was received by the Coast Guard a day and a half after the sinking, and (3) lifesaving equipment on the SS MORRELL did not provide the weather protection necessary for survival under existing weather and sea conditions.

BY THE NATIONAL TRANSPORTATION SAFETY BOARD:

/s/ Joseph J. O'Connell, Jr., Chairman

/s/ Oscar M. Laurel, Member

/s/ John H. Reed, Member

/s/ Louis M. Thayer, Member

/s/ Francis H. McAdams, Member

The letter of recommendation to the Coast Guard is attached.

DEPARTMENT OF TRANSPORTATION

NATIONAL TRANSPORTATION SAFETY BOARD

WASHINGTON, D.C. 20591

February 8, 1968

————————o————————

Admiral Willard J. Smith,
Commandant, U. S. Coast Guard,
Washington, D. C. 20591.

Dear Admiral Smith:

In reviewing the Marine Board of Investigation on the sinking of the SS DANIEL J. MORRELL, and your action on that report, the National Transportation Safety Board is concerned that a similar tragedy may occur to other bulk carriers under similar circumstances. The fractures sustained by the sister ship SS EDWARD Y. TOWNSEND in the same vicinity and under like conditions substantiate this concern. Another example is the breaking and sinking of the SS CARL D. BRADLEY in Lake Michigan on November 18, 1958, which was attributed to an undetected structural weakness or defect.

In the MORRELL case, the recommendations of the Marine Board should adequately cope with emergencies resulting from fractures and other accidents in these vessels. We are also concerned with measures to prevent the failure of the hull girder in vessels of that general type.

We share your interest and responsibility for the prevention of accidents. Accordingly, we request a summary of the results of your special inspections of the older Great Lakes vessels, and of joint studies now in process, at an early date. In addition, information is requested concerning current plans for construction of replacement vessels, which seems to be the ultimate solution to this problem. A list of the current U. S. Great Lakes bulk carrier fleet, giving date of construction, size, owner, and other significant data would also be helpful to the Board.

While we fully appreciate the economic aspects involved in methods that would help prevent failure of hull girders, from a safety standpoint, we recommend that you consider further action as follows:

A. Strengthen the deck and/or sheer strake structure in the midships area in vessels over 400 feet long constructed prior to 1948, or curtail the operation of these vessels during specific days and period of the fall season when adverse weather and wave conditions approach or exceed those encountered by the SS DANIEL J. MORRELL.

B. Based on the special inspection program, implement a progressive structural renewal program on an individual ship basis.

The Safety Board recognizes the efforts of all those involved in the research and study of the forces and effects of sea and weather on the safety of vessels, and urges the continuation and intensification of such studies to develop objective technical criteria relating hull structural integrity to weather, sea, and other conditions of operation.[1]

---

1 The Chairman and Members McAdams and Laurel concur in the observations made with respect to the desirability of the continuation and intensification of efforts to develop better objective criteria relating to hull structural integrity, but wish still further to stress and amplify on the importance of such a program.

Specifically, they have this to say:

"Completely adequate information was not available to the master of the SS MORRELL as to the hull strength of his vessel under temperature and sea conditions forecast and observable at the time he determined to leave port. As you know, the master of another vessel of nearly identical design also left port and proceeded in the vicinity of the SS MORRELL under identical temperature and sea conditions and was fractured in the same manner; but to a lesser degree. Both ships, however, had exceeded the margins of fracture resistance and it seems clear that the master of neither ship had reason to expect what happened. We recognize that efforts are constantly being made by the Coast Guard and private organizations to learn more of the forces and effects of sea and weather on the safety of vessels, and it is apparent that this tragedy has resulted in a continuation and intensification of them.

This Board concurs in the recommendations contained in the MORRELL report, and urges implementation of them prior to the next shipping season, along with our recommendation to provide emergency lighting in the forward quarters and life-raft embarkation location. The need for a position-reporting system is considered of prime importance, and voluntary compliance by the Great Lakes operators should be obtained prior to next season.

Sincerely,

s/ Joseph J. O'Connell, Jr.,

Chairman

"However, we wish to emphasize that even had the master of the SS MOR-RELL had all the currently available information concerning the basic structural integrity of the vessel under sea conditions, temperature and loading conditions existing immediately prior to the accident, he would still have been unable to make an intelligent judgment as to the hull integrity of the vessel under the then existing conditions. Under the conditions here present, the master could have estimated the sea conditions but could not have estimated the ability of the vessel to meet them, and therefore we are of the belief that special efforts seem warranted to develop information better calculated to provide a master with data useful and, in this case, vital to intelligent decisions."

DEPARTMENT OF TRANSPORTATION

UNITED STATES COAST GUARD

Address reply to:
COMMANDANT (MVI-3)
U.S. COAST GUARD
WASHINGTON, D.C.
20591

5943/DANIEL J. MORRELL
A-9 Bd
4 OCT 1967

Commandant's Action

on

The Marine Board of Investigation convened to investigate
the sinking of the SS DANIEL J. MORRELL in Lake Huron
with loss of life on 29 November 1966

The record of the Marine Board of Investigation convened to
investigate subject casualty has been reviewed and the record, including the Findings of Fact, Conclusions and Recommendations, is approved subject to the final determination
of the cause of the casualty by the National Transportation
Safety Board and the following comments.

REMARKS

1. The Coast Guard instituted a review immediately after this
casualty looking into every Great Lakes bulk cargo vessel
structural failure since 1956. The review considered vessel age, section modulus, length to depth ratio, structural
changes, repowering, location of the failure together with
the circumstances of the failure including the prevailing air
temperature. This review served to pinpoint those vessels of
the Great Lakes bulk cargo vessel fleet that warranted particular examination for possible incipient fractures or other

indications of structural weakness. Sixteen such vessels were examined for incipient fractures primarily in the critical area of midships hatch corners. Two were found to be in need of corrective action. Corrective action was taken on one vessel. The other vessel remains in a laid-up status and will require corrective action before being permitted to return to operation. This program was then extended and is continuing to include additional vessels. One of the results of the program has been the development of a relatively simple non-destructive method of examining concealed portions of the main deck stringer plating in way of hatch coamings.

2. In order that the magnitude of the dynamic forces involved may be better understood, a number of comprehensive scientific studies have been underway for a considerable period of time. With the close participation of the Coast Guard, The Society of Naval Architects and Marine Engineers have been working on the following projects.

a. In cooperation with a number of government agencies of both the United States and Canada, the Society is conducting a detailed study of Great Lakes wave action. Analysis of results of observations for 1965 and 1966 is expected before the end of 1967.

b. A U. S. Great Lakes bulk cargo vessel has been provided with stress measuring and recording equipment which will make available a determination of the dynamic forces to which the vessel's hull is subject during all stages of her operation. Stress data is available for 1965 and 1966, and will be available for part of 1967. This information will be correlated with wave data obtained by means of radio wave buoys recorded in 1966 and with the further data being recorded for 1967. The Canadian Government is also conducting similar studies and has several vessels so instrumented.

c. Models of 700 foot and projected 1000 foot Great Lakes vessels are now being tested. The information obtained in the wave data and the vessel stress project will be correlated with the model basin tests.

3. A joint Canadian-U. S. Great Lakes Load Lines Technical Committee has been established by the Coast Guard and the Canadian Board of Steamship Inspection. The objective of this Committee will be to determine the strength, freeboard and other requirements pertinent to the assignment of applicable vessel load lines. This Committee will utilize the latest and most up-to-date scientific information. It is expected that the groups working on these studies will make a worthwhile contribution to a better understanding of the problems of adequate hull strength.

4. In order to determine the cause of the casualty as fully as possible the Board had the benefit of underwater diving and television picture relays on the sunken stern section. In addition, a large section of the sheerstrake and a small section of deck plate were recovered and subjected to metallurgical study. This enabled the Board to determine that the fracture sustained was "brittle fracture typical of many prior ship fractures in pre-1948 steel." However, while the fracture was clearly of brittle-type, it differed from fractures previously noted in welded ships in that it progressed through a transverse line of rivet holes. Thus, the rivet holes clearly were not effective as crack arrestors. In the case of the sheerstrake fracture a rivet hole was identified as a fracture source.

ACTION CONCERNING THE RECOMMENDATIONS

1. The Board's recommendations concerning providing inflatable liferafts, emergency source of power for radio communication, and modifications to the general alarm system are being given prompt consideration by the Coast Guard and will be submitted to the Merchant Marine Council for consideration of implementing regulations. Insofar as the emergency source of power for radio communication is concerned this recommendation is being considered in cooperation and in conjunction with the Federal Communications Commission which has indicated its support of the recommendation.

2. The Board's recommendation that future Great Lakes bulk cargo vessels be constructed with sufficient compartmentation so that the vessel can remain afloat even if any one main cargo hold is flooded, warrants consideration and study. All organizations and individuals interested in safety on the Great Lakes must be concerned with casualties such as this and the loss due to the collision of the CEDARVILLE and TOPDALSFJORD in May 1965. In that casualty, the TOPDALSFJORD struck the fully laden CEDARVILLE amidships at nearly a right angle. Once the main cargo hold was breached by collision and the flooding could not be controlled, the vessel's sinking was inevitable. It seems that the departures from present design and construction which would be necessary to provide an effective degree of compartmentation may be small enough to be justifiable having regard to economics as well as safety. Accordingly, the Coast Guard will undertake to consult with other interested organizations looking to the feasibility of such a design.

3. The Board recommended evaluation of the need for tarpaulins on vessels equipped with secured sliding plate type hatch covers during all seasons when not carrying cargo. Since this involves an amendment to the existing load line regulations, the recommendation will be forwarded by the Coast Guard to the joint Canadian-U. S. Great Lakes Load Lines Technical Committee for consideration and evaluation.

4. The Board's recommendation concerning providing the Master of a Great Lakes bulk cargo vessel with a loading manual that would indicate the limiting longitudinal bending moment factor that his vessel can safely sustain will likewise be presented to the joint Canadian-U. S. Great Lakes Load Lines Technical Committee.

5. The absence of a distress message precluded prompt institution of search and rescue efforts. Therefore, the recommendation that vessels be provided with a datum marker buoy has considerable merit. This subject has been under discussion and study by the Maritime Safety Committee of the

Inter-Governmental Maritime Consultative Organization for some time. There is now international agreement on the characteristics and frequencies of such marine emergency position indicating radio beacon. Therefore, the Coast Guard will undertake a study in consultation with concerned industry representatives, government agencies and others to determine whether this emergency radio beacon should be required on United States vessels. In the interim the voluntary equipping of Great Lakes vessels with the device is encouraged.

The record indicates that the owners of the DANIEL J. MORRELL had in effect a daily reporting system during certain periods of the operating season. The Board's recommendation that when a vessel fails to report as scheduled positive action should be instituted by the persons concerned has been presented to the owners and operators. This positive action should include early notification to the Coast Guard in order that their search and rescue facilities may be alerted while the vessel's owners continue to try to determine the status of the vessel. This early notification, preferably within one hour, will enable all facilities at hand to be more promptly utilized.

6. A copy of the Board's report will be forwarded by the Coast Guard to the Environmental Science Services Administration of the U. S. Department of Commerce for study and consideration of the recommendation that on-scene sea conditions be reported in regular marine weather broadcasts. Preliminary discussions with personnel of that agency have been held.

7. Concerning the reported separation of the signal pistol, Coast Guard casualty statistics do not indicate a similar failure of a signal pistol screw such as is reported to have occurred. Accordingly, in lieu of an amendment to the regulations governing the construction of this signal pistol, the Coast Guard has taken steps to carefully examine these pistols at subsequent vessel equipment inspections in order to determine if similar conditions exist. In addition,

the manufacturers of currently approved signal pistols have
been advised of the necessity for adequate securing of these
screws.

CONCLUDING REMARKS

1. While every effort is being taken to prevent recurrence of
this type of casualty, the magnitude of the problem must be
recognized in order that the corrective steps taken or con-
templated or subsequently deemed necessary may be understood
within the parameters of the situation as it exists. The
average age of the Great Lakes bulk carrier fleet is about 45
years. There are more vessels in the 50 to 60 year age group
than any other 10 year period. These vessels are constructed
of a type of steel which has not been used in large vessel
construction since 1948. This pre-1948 steel generally has a
high transition temperature, and is therefore susceptible to
brittle fracture. While it is true that corrosion of steel
under the fresh water conditions of the Great Lakes is minimal, fatigue as a result of repeated stress cycling over a
long period of years can and does result in local structural deterioration in the form of fatigue cracks. This type
of deterioration may be difficult to detect despite diligent
inspection. Because of these conditions it must be recognized
that the remedial steps necessary to reduce the possibility
of a recurrence of this tragedy must involve all groups concerned. The vessel's loading, discharge and ballasting must
be such as to minimize stress. Full allowance and consideration must be given to the restrictions that adverse weather
will place upon the vessel. The operation, maintenance and
husbanding of the vessel must at all times give full rec-
ognition to these factors and therefrom result in prudent,
careful operating procedures and practices. Safe operation of
the present Great Lakes fleet will require the efforts of all
groups and individuals concerned.

W. J. SMITH
Admiral, U. S. Coast Guard
Commandant

———————•———————

From: Marine Board of Investigation
To: Commandant (MVI)

Subj: SS DANIEL J. MORRELL, O.N. 203507, sinking of
      in Lake Huron on 29 November 1966, with loss
      of life

FINDINGS OF FACT

1. At approximately 0200, EST, 29 November 1966, while en
route from Buffalo, N. Y. to Taconite, Minnesota in ballast,
the SS DANIEL J. MORRELL, broke into two sections during the
height of a storm and sank in Lake Huron in the approximate
position of latitude 44°15.9'N and 82°50'W. At the time of
the sinking neither lifeboat was launched and no distress
message was transmitted by that vessel. The first notification of alarm for her safety was received by the U. S. Coast
Guard Rescue Coordination Center at Cleveland, Ohio at 12:15
EST, 30 November 1966. Of the 29 crew members on board at the
time, 22 are known dead, 6 are still missing and one person
survived. U. S. Lake Survey, Lake Huron Chart No. 5 encom-
passes the area.

2. The following are the particulars of the vessel involved:

Name:	DANIEL J. MORRELL
Official Number:	203507
Service:	Freight
Structural Form:	Typical Great Lakes bulk freighter
Gross tons:	7,763
Net tons:	6,216

Length:	586.5'
Breadth:	58.2'
Depth:	27.4'
Propulsion:	Steam, single screw, Skinner Unaflow, three cylinder, 2 coal fired water-tube Babcock and Wilcox boilers.
Horsepower:	3,200
Home Port:	Cleveland, Ohio
Where Built:	West Bay City, Michigan
Date Built:	1906
Owners:	Cambria Steamship Company 2600 Terminal Tower Cleveland, Ohio 44113
Operators:	Bethlehem Steel Company Great Lakes Steamship Division 2600 Terminal Tower Cleveland, Ohio 44113
Master:	Arthur I. Crawley 2725 Lakeview Avenue Rocky River, Ohio 44116
License:	114142
Certificate:	Z-782585

Last Drydock Inspection:
Date:	25 February 1966
Port:	Toledo, Ohio

Last Annual Inspection for Certification:
Date:	15 April 1966
Port:	Toledo, Ohio

Date Certificate of Inspection Issued: 15 April 1966

Last Midseason Inspection:
Date:	20 July 1966
Port:	Buffalo, N.Y.
Classification:	American Bureau of Shipping - Maltese cross A1 Great Lakes Service, Maltese cross AMS - Classification being maintained at time of sinking

3. The following crew members, who lost their lives as a result of this casualty, have been recovered and positively identified:

Name	Capacity	Next of Kin
Arthur I. Crawley, age 47	Master	Mrs. Mary C. Reidy, Sister
Phillip E. Kapets, age 51	1st Mate	Mrs. Florence E. Kapets, Wife
Duncan R. MacLeod, age 61	2nd Mate	Mrs. Catherine R. MacLeod, Wife
Charles M. Fosbender, age 42	Wheelsman	Mrs. Janice B. Fosbender, Wife
Henry Rischmiller, age 34	Wheelsman	Mrs. Claudia Rischmiller, Mother
Stuart A. Campbell, age 60	Wheelsman	Mrs. Vera M. Campbell, Wife
Albert P. Whoeme, age 51	Watchman	Mrs. Ethel P. Whoeme, Wife
Norman M. Bragg, age 40	Watchman	Mrs. Louise V. Bragg, Mother
Larry G. Davis, age 27	Ordinary Deckwatch	Mrs. Joyce A. Davis, Wife
Arthur E. Stojek, age 41	Deckhand	Mrs. Cecelia A. Stojek, Wife
John J. Cleary, Jr., age 20	Deckhand	Mr. John J. Cleary, Sr., Father
John H. Schmidt, age 46	Chief Engineer	Mrs. Helen F. Schmidt, Wife
Valmour A. Marchildon, age 43	1st Asst. Engineer	Mrs. Fleurette A. Marchildon, Wife
Wilson E. Simpson, age 50	Oiler	Mr. Charlie W. Simpson, Brother

Name	Capacity	Next of Kin
Arthur S. Fargo, age 52	Fireman	Mrs. Nellie Fargo, Wife
Chester Konieczka, age 45	Fireman	Mr. Edward Kane, Brother
Leon R. Truman, age 45	Coalpasser	Mrs. Genevieve M. Truman, Wife
Nicholas Homick, age 35	2nd Cook	Mrs. Helen Welgo, Sister
Joseph A. Mahsem, age 59	Porter	Mrs. Brian Eide, Daughter
Charles J. Sestakauskas, age 49	Porter	Mrs. Anna E. Sestakauskas
George A. Dahl, age 38	3rd Asst. Engineer	Mrs. Dorothy M. Dahl, Wife
Saverio Grippi, age 53	Coalpasser	Mrs. Sarah Grippi, Wife

4. The following crewmembers aboard the DANIEL J. MORRELL at the time of sinking are still missing:

Name	Capacity	Next of Kin
Ernest G. Marcotte, age 62	3rd Mate	Mrs. Ruthie J. Marcotte, Wife
John M. Groh, age 21	Ordinary-Deckwatch	Mrs. Louise Groh, Mother
Alfred G. Norkunas, age 39	2nd Asst. Engineer	Mrs. Marilyn R. Norkunas, Wife
Donald E. Worcester, age 38	Oiler	Mrs. Judith Worcester, Wife
David L. Price, age 19	Coalpasser	Mr. W. L. Price, Father
Stanley J. Satlawa, age 39	Steward	Mr. Edward F. Satlawa, Brother

5. The following crewmember of the DANIEL J. MORRELL is the only survivor of this casualty:

Name and Address	Capacity
Dennis N. Hale, age 26	Watchman

6. All Merchant Mariner's Documents that have been recovered in this case have been forwarded under separate cover.

7. The weather in the general area of the casualty was: seas 20 to 25 feet, northerly to north northeast; visibility 4 miles; sea temperature 44° to 47°F; air temperature 33°F; barometer 29.10. A recording of the wind by the Harbor Beach Coast Guard Station, as taken from a Weather Bureau Wind Recorder, indicated that the wind was variable from 2200, 28 November 1966 to 0500, 29 November 1966, ranging from 30 knots to 57 knots and gusty, shifting back and forth from northwest to east. At 0128, 29 November, the wind shifted from northwest over to east northeast and except for a period of about five minutes when it shifted to northwest, it generally remained from that direction until 0207. At about 0200 the wind velocity was 35 to 40 knots, with gusts to 57 knots. Further information regarding weather conditions is indicated in succeeding paragraphs.

8. The weather forecast for Lake Huron as originated by the Weather Bureau, Chicago, Illinois, and broadcast to become effective at 1200 EST, 28 November 1966, was:

a. Gale warnings. For the northern one-third, north-easterly winds 34 to 40 knots the first six hours, becoming northerly 34 to 40 knots, occasionally northerly 41 to 47 knots the following 12 hours and north-westerly winds 28 to 33 knots the following six hours.

b. For the southern two-thirds, westerly winds 34 to 40 knots the first six hours, northwesterly winds 41 to 47 knots the following 12 hours, with winds diminishing northwesterly

28 to 33 knots the following six hours. The weather for the entire period snow, or rain and snow the entire 24 hour period.

c. The forecast effective 1800 EST, 28 November 1966, was: Gale warnings continued in effect. Northerly winds 28 to 33 knots at the beginning of the period but increasing to 34 to 40 knots, occasionally gusty, or occasionally 41 to 47 knots and snow, or rain and snow for the entire 24 hours.

d. The forecast effective 0000 EST, 29 November 1966 was: Gale warnings continued in effect, with northerly wind 41 to 47 knots for the entire 24 hours; snow, or rain and snow the entire 24 hour period.

9. The DANIEL J. MORRELL was a non self-unloading bulk freighter. The forepeak, or collision, and the after peak bulkheads were watertight. The blind hold bulkhead at the forward end of the No. 1 cargo hold and the after bulkhead of No. 3 cargo hold were watertight to the main deck. There were no doors in the watertight bulkheads below the main deck level. The main deck was at the level of the side tank tops. Two non-watertight screen bulkheads separated the three cargo holds. Openings were located at the port and starboard corners of the screen bulkheads at the tank top level for drainage purposes. Water was removed from the cargo spaces by means of suctions at the port and starboard after corners of the No. 3 cargo hold. Water could be pumped into the cargo hold through this same piping arrangement.

10. There were 14 combination side and double bottomed tanks, 7 on each side of the center vertical keel. The exact capacity of any of the ballast tanks is unknown; however, the capacity of each tank was approximately 8.5 short tons per foot of length. The feed water tank was located below the engine spaces. The hull was of riveted construction and the vessel was transversely framed. There were 18 hatches with sliding steel type hatch covers and Mulholland hatch securing clamps. The hatches were on 24 foot centers. The dimensions of the

hatches were 12 feet by 36 feet. In 1942, new side tanks were installed. In 1945 the vessel was re-boilered, with boilers constructed by Babcock and Wilcox Company. In 1956 new plate tank tops were installed, at which time there was much renewal of steel internals. In 1956 the vessel was repowered with a Skinner Unaflow engine of 3200 H.P. Prior to being re-powered the old engine plant was triple expansion steam of 2000 H.P. The Skinner Unaflow engine was of lighter weight than the engine previously installed. The old shaft was 12 inches in diameter, the new shaft diameter was 14 inches, the old propeller was of 4 bladed cast iron construction and the new propeller was 5 bladed. The maximum speed of the vessel increased approximately 2½ to 3 m.p.h., but there was a little more vibration noticeable subsequent to the new engine installation. A former Chief Engineer of the DANIEL J. MORRELL knew of no problems created by the installation of the Skinner Unaflow engine.

11. The berthing quarters for deck officers and personnel were located forward. Quarters for all other personnel were located aft.

12. The lifesaving equipment on the DANIEL J. MORRELL included two 21 person lifeboats aft and two 15 person liferafts; one raft located on the spar deck between No. 3 and 4 hatches and the other located on the boat deck aft. The boats were of steel construction, built by the Welin Davit and Boat Corporation. Davits were of the sheath screw type. Lifeboat releasing gear consisted of common hooks. Boat falls were wire rope. There were no electric boat winches aboard. The lifesaving equipment provided no means of protecting personnel from exposure. The liferafts were of wood and metal construction, built by Frank Morrison, Inc., and were the catamaran float free type.

13. The power for the general alarm system consisted of dry cell batteries located both forward and aft. The alarm switch was located in the pilothouse, and once the switch was engaged, the alarm would continue to ring forward and aft.

In event the wiring was severed aft of the forward superstructure, the alarm bells aft would not ring. The source of
electrical power for all other units on the vessel was two 60
KW Westinghouse generators which were located adjacent to the
main throttle. There was no emergency lighting system on the
vessel, although there were battery powered battle lanterns
aboard.

14. There was one AM and one FM radio installation located
in the pilothouse, with remote stations for each located in
the Captain's cabin. There was no emergency radio aboard. The
vessel was equipped with a radio direction finder and radar.
Steam piping and electrical cable were installed immediately
below the spar deck on the starboard side. There was no public address system aboard. The vessel was equipped with sound
powered phones and engine order telegraph for communication
between the engineroom and pilothouse. Wires and cables for
these systems were also located beneath the spar deck starboard side.

15. There was no cargo loading plan prepared by Bethlehem
Steel Corporation, nor is one required by regulations. Vessel operating personnel, however, believe that the procedure
generally used is one which produces the least strain on the
hull structure. As the cargo is admitted into the holds the
ballast is removed. The chief mate plans the loading of each
cargo. His usual procedure is to put partial loads in hatch
18 and then in even number hatches proceeding forward. Then
partial cargoes are loaded in the odd numbered hatches starting with number 17. Additional cargo is distributed in the
hatches until the completion of loading.

16. The DANIEL J. MORRELL departed Buffalo, New York for
Taconite, Minnesota on 26 November 1966 and cleared the Buffalo breakwater at 2300 EST that date. She was on her 34th
and last scheduled voyage of the 1966 operating season. The
vessel was in a ballasted condition at the time of departure
because of known rough weather existing in Lake Erie. There
is no record of the exact distribution of ballast or drafts

upon her departure. The fleet Engineer for Bethlehem Steel Corporation observed the vessel at the time of her departure from Buffalo and was aware of no vessel structural defects at that time.

17. In accordance with company policy requiring all vessels of the Bethlehem Fleet to communicate with a company dispatcher at Cleveland to make daily position reports during early Spring and late Fall, at or about 0900, 27 November 1966, Captain Crawley called Mr. Dobson, the dispatcher, by radio telephone and reported that he was due at Detroit about 1830 to 1900, 27 November. On the evening of 27 November 1966, Captain Crawley called to report that the DANIEL J. MORRELL had anchored below Detroit, Michigan at 1800 due to adverse weather. At about 0900, 28 November 1966, Captain Crawley called Mr. Dobson again to report that he had heaved anchor at 0655, 28 November 1966, that he had passed Detroit and that he was short two deck hands and one fireman. At the time of sinking, the vessel was actually one fireman and one oiler short of the crew required by the Certificate of Inspection. It is noted, however, that the vessel was carrying more crew in number than was required. There were no further conversations or contacts between the master of the DANIEL J. MORRELL and company officials in Cleveland, Ohio; and no report or notification from any source was received to indicate there might have been any problems on board the DANIEL J. MORRELL from the last radio contact at 0900, 28 November 1966, until the time of sinking.

18. Upon departing Buffalo, the DANIEL J. MORRELL had orders to stop for fuel (coal) at the Consolidation Fuel Dock (Mullen Dock), Windsor, Ontario, Canada, in event fuel was required. The DANIEL J. MORRELL did arrive at the above dock at 0705, 28 November 1966 and, after taking on 221 tons of stoker fuel, departed at 0730. No draft reading of the vessel was taken by dock personnel. The ETA of the DANIEL J. MORRELL at Taconite was about 2100, 29 November 1966, barring unexpected delays. The J. W. Westcott Company, Detroit, Michigan,

an automatic reporting station for Bethlehem Fleet vessels passing Detroit, reported that the DANIEL J. MORRELL passed Detroit upbound at 0753 on 28 November 1966.

19. The smooth log of the DANIEL J. MORRELL, covering previous trips in 1966, indicates its usual ballasted condition upon departure from Buffalo without cargo, as was the case on 26 November 1966, was approximately 8 to 10 feet forward and 16 to 17 feet aft, depending on weather conditions. Testimony from the DANIEL J. MORRELL's previous master, Captain Hull, indicated that this ballasting procedure as carried out by Captain Crawley followed basically his own ballasting procedures while on that vessel. In good weather he normally carried about six feet of water in #1, #2 and #3 tanks and about 8 to 10 feet in the after tanks. Then as the weather increased in severity, he would fill all ballast tanks in an attempt to increase his draft forward and aft. All tanks were filled simultaneously while the vessel was at unloading ports. A draft of 14'8" aft was sufficient to submerge subject vessel's propeller completely. Bethlehem Steel Corporation dispatchers designated the ports at which vessels are to load and unload bulk cargo and the cargoes to be carried. The determination as to whether or not a vessel will proceed in the face of a storm is in the province of the master. The cargoes carried by the DANIEL J. MORRELL were coal, rock (limestone), and Taconite.

20. The EDWARD Y. TOWNSEND, also of the Bethlehem Fleet and a sister ship of the DANIEL J. MORRELL, was moored astern of the DANIEL J. MORRELL at the Bethlehem Steel Plant, Buffalo, New York, at the time of the latter vessel's departure from Buffalo. The EDWARD Y. TOWNSEND departed Buffalo for Taconite Harbor, Minnesota at 0310, 27 November 1966 in ballast. Captain Thomas J. Connelly was master of that vessel. At approximately 2310, 27 November, the upbound EDWARD Y. TOWNSEND passed the MORRELL while it was anchored in the Detroit River below Detroit, Michigan. At that time, the masters of the two vessels engaged in radio conversation concerning the weather

conditions in Lake Huron and the intention of the master of
the EDWARD Y. TOWNSEND to anchor in upper St. Clair River
to await more favorable weather. The EDWARD Y. TOWNSEND then
continued upbound and anchored below Stag Island in the St.
Clair River at 0400, 28 November 1966. The next communication with the DANIEL J. MORRELL was at about 1300, 28 November 1966 as it passed the anchored EDWARD Y. TOWNSEND. The
two masters discussed the noon weather report for Lake Huron
and the weather that might be anticipated. The wind at Stag
Island at that time was estimated as westerly and light (6 to
18 miles per hour).

21. Prior to heaving anchor at 1453, the master of the
EDWARD Y. TOWNSEND listened to radio conversations between unidentified vessels in Lake Huron and to shore station radio broadcasts, to get some indication of on-scene
weather in the southern part of Lake Huron. The wind in the
southern part of Lake Huron was westerly and light to fresh
(6 to 28 miles per hour). Immediately prior to his heaving
anchor, the masters of the TOWNSEND and the MORRELL again
conferred by radio. At this time the DANIEL J. MORRELL was
in the vicinity of the Lake Huron Lightship. The conversation generally concerned weather conditions. The next conversation between the two vessels was at about the time the
EDWARD Y. TOWNSEND was abeam of Harbor Beach. That vessel
logged Harbor Beach Breakwater Light abeam at 2028 at a distance of 4.3 miles and the master was attempting to follow
the recommended upbound track as indicated on Lake Survey
Chart No. 5. The DANIEL J. MORRELL was ahead of the EDWARD Y.
TOWNSEND, proceeding upbound at this time but her exact position is unknown. Again, general weather conditions were
discussed. At this time the wind was northerly, at about 35
miles per hour and increasing rapidly. The sea was estimated to be northerly eight feet and building up. Distance
between crests was approximately 250 to 300 feet. The next
communication between the two vessels was at about 2200 and
concerned the deteriorating weather and sea conditions and
courses of the two vessels. The wind was still northerly

and had increased to about 50 miles per hour. The seas were
then 12 feet and northerly. The EDWARD Y. TOWNSEND, although
riding fairly well to this point, had started to pound and
roll. Captain Connelly restricted movement of personnel
between the forward and after sections of the vessel from
2200, 28 November until 2200, 29 November 1966 because of
the fear of broaching. Captain Crawley indicated that he was
steering 347°T in order to make good 341°T, the recommended
upbound course. There was further radiotelephone communication at about 2315 and at this time the wind had increased
to an estimated 50 to 55 miles per hour and the seas were
still building up. Until this time the EDWARD Y. TOWNSEND
had experienced no difficulty in steering or holding into
the sea. While on Lake Huron the EDWARD Y. TOWNSEND carried
nine feet of water in #1 port and starboard tanks. All other
ballast tanks were full except that the after peak tank was
filled to within approximately one foot of the top. The master of that vessel had considered proceeding to Thunder Bay
to anchor in protected waters and had discussed this possibility with Captain Crawley. An alternative which had been
discussed by the two masters earlier was whether to return
to Port Huron. Captain Connelly deemed it safer to head into
the sea. He stated that there would be more twisting action
of his vessel in a quartering sea and expressed the fear of
broaching and not being able to get his light vessel out of
the trough. At about 2350, 28 November 1966, Captain Crawley
called the EDWARD Y. TOWNSEND. The master of the latter vessel said, "I will call you back," and hung up the phone. At
the time of the call the EDWARD Y. TOWNSEND had just started to blow around or broach into the seas. The vessel fell
off to starboard approximately 22 degrees before it could
be brought back on course with left full rudder. At approximately 0015, 29 November 1966, Captain Connelly called
Captain Crawley. At this time Captain Crawley indicated that
the DANIEL J. MORRELL had just had a similar experience to
that of the EDWARD Y. TOWNSEND, in that his vessel had also
been blown off course. This conversation was brief because
both masters were busy attenuating to hold the two vessels

into the sea. At no time did Captain Crawley indicate what
his exact plans were concerning vessel operations or itin-
erary. This was the last known contact with the DANIEL J.
MORRELL. From the time of the DANIEL J. MORRELL's departure
from Buffalo, New York on 26 November 1966 through the last
communication with the EDWARD Y. TOWNSEND at 0015, 29 November 1966, the master of the DANIEL J. MORRELL had not
reported any difficulty with his vessel, radios, equipment,
structure, operations, machinery, or problems of any kind
except weather conditions and the difficulty of holding the
vessel into the sea.

22. Communications between the two vessels through the time
of the last contact had been normal. Channel 16 (156.8 Mcs.)
(FM) had been used as calling frequency and channels 6 and
8 (156.3 Mcs. and 156.4 Mcs.) (FM) were used in conducting
radio conversation at all times between the two vessels.
Channel 51, the calling and distress frequency (2182 kc.)
or channel 52, (2003 kcs.), the working frequency for the
AM radio, had not been used between the two vessels. The
EDWARD Y. TOWNSEND was maintaining a continuous listening
watch on channel 51.

23. Captain Connelly estimated the wind to be northerly at
65 miles per hour at 0015 and described the seas as "tremendous." The height of the seas was 20 feet and the distance between crests was still 250 to 300 feet. By 0200 the
wind was about 65 miles per hour and had shifted to the
north-northeast. Seas had built up to about 25 feet. The
EDWARD Y. TOWNSEND was pitching, rolling and pounding at
this time but even though there was difficulty experienced
in holding her into the sea, she did not fall off more than
approximately 25 degrees and did not roll more than approximately 20 degrees. During the height of the storm some solid water was taken over the bow. At approximately 0145 and
again at about 0345, Captain Connelly attempted radio contact
with the DANIEL J. MORRELL without success. He attributed
this failure to make radio contact to radio problems on the

MORRELL. The radar on board the EDWARD Y. TOWNSEND had been turned on at approximately 1800, 28 November 1966, but at no time was there known radar contact with the DANIEL J. MORRELL and she was not sighted visually. No attempt was actually made to establish radar contact with that vessel.

24. Captain Connelly could not give an accurate distance separating the two vessels subsequent to the heaving of the anchor by the EDWARD Y. TOWNSEND at 1453, 28 November 1966. His best estimate was that 20 miles separated the two vessels at that time and that the distance probably had shortened by the time of the casualty because the DANIEL J. MORRELL had experienced adverse weather earlier.

25. The last estimated position of the EDWARD Y. TOWNSEND prior to 0200, 29 November 1966, was 066°T and 7.7 miles from Point Aux Barques Light, at 2350. The master was attempting to follow the recommended charted trackline of 341°True. He indicated that at 0200 the vessel would have made good approximately three miles from the 2350 position.

26. From the time of passing the Lake Huron Lightship until 2028, 28 November the EDWARD Y. TOWNSEND was able to make turns that would normally give her 13.9 miles per hour over the bottom and was making good approximately 13.3 m.p.h. when it passed abeam of the Harbor Beach Breakwater Light. Due to weather conditions, Captain Connelly had to reduce speed to 90 revolutions per minute at 2045 and 75 revolutions per minute at 2050, which would give him approximately 10 and 8 miles per hour over the bottom respectively under normal conditions. His vessel was making an estimated 5 to 6 miles per hour at 2050. By 2350, the vessel was making about two miles per hour over the bottom. After 2350 it was necessary occasionally to increase to full speed to keep the vessel's bow from falling off; and the engineers automatically reduced RPM when the propeller came out of the water. This occurred at approximately two minute intervals. Thereafter the engineers attempted to maintain 80 RPM.

27. By 1130, 29 November 1966, the winds had diminished to approximately 50 to 55 miles per hour. At 1400, 29 November 1966, the EDWARD Y. TOWNSEND, after gradually changing course to head into the wind and sea, was at an estimated position of 56.3 miles bearing 203°True from Cove Island Radio Beacon. The master of the EDWARD Y. TOWNSEND found the wind and sea conditions in the area off Point Aux Barques more severe than anticipated as a result of weather forecasts and on-scene weather in the lower two-thirds of Lake Huron prior to his passing Lake Huron Lightship. He could not recall having experienced sea conditions of this magnitude on the Great Lakes. He expressed the opinion that he could not have lowered his boats safely had such action been necessary.

28. On 29 November, water was discovered in the cargo holds of the TOWNSEND to a depth of approximately 45 inches at the after bulkhead. This water extended forward to the mid cargo hold length. The master was surprised to discover such a quantity of water because none had been pumped into the holds intentionally. This quantity of water was attributed to side tank leakage since the time of departing Buffalo. A former third mate of the DANIEL J. MORRELL stated that the only water normally found in the cargo hold was the result of leakage from the ballast tanks. The only times that he has seen a considerable tonnage of water in the cargo holds of Great Lakes bulk carriers was when water was placed in the holds deliberately. He stated that carriage of such water in the holds as ballast was a normal Great Lakes practice. He expressed the belief that if too much water is carried in the cargo holds the hatches may be damaged by water impact as the vessel rolls.

29. A former master of the DANIEL J. MORRELL testified that he has pumped water into cargo holds when in heavy seas in order to keep the propeller submerged. He believed that this cargo hold ballast would make the ship more stable. He would, however, limit the depth of water to three feet at the after cargo hold bulkhead. The reason expressed for this form of

ballasting was that the propeller must be kept submerged in order to prevent damage to propulsion machinery.

30. Tarpaulins were not installed over the sliding plate type hatch covers of the EDWARD Y. TOWNSEND on 28 or 29 November 1966. The master stated that this type hatch cover leaks very little and that tarpaulins are normally used during Spring and Fall months when the vessel is loaded with cargo. The previous master of the DANIEL J. MORRELL stated that he does not require tarpaulins to be installed over the hatch covers when there is no cargo aboard, even in bad weather.

31. On 30 November 1966 the EDWARD Y. TOWNSEND stopped for fuel at Lime Island in the Lower St. Mary's River. At this time the master received a report that there were some loose rivets in the deck plating, starboard side, weather deck (spar deck). Upon further inspection, it was found that there was a crack extending from the forward starboard corner of number 10 hatch to and running beneath the deck strap which is located between the hatches and the sheer strake, starboard side. Prior to this time the master was not aware of any structural damages. Normal working and springing had been experienced but it was not considered excessive. The damages were reported to the company officials who in turn made the required report to the Coast Guard.

32. The M/V BENSON FORD, having anchored at Bois Blanc Island, Straits of Mackinac, because of weather conditions, heaved anchor at 0850 EST, 28 November 1966, and proceeded downbound into Lake Huron. The loaded vessel was basically following the recommended downbound track line. At the time of heaving anchor there was a northerly gale. The log book for the BENSON FORD indicated that she passed Presque Isle at 1509 EST at which time the wind was NNE whole gale. The passing of Thunder Bay Island was logged at 1800 and wind was NNE whole gale. Log book entries from 1947, 28 November to 0702, 29 November 1966, the time of arrival of that vessel at Lake Huron Lightship, indicated northerly whole gale winds. The master of the BENSON FORD estimated that the storm was at its

greatest intensity between the hours of 2200, 28 November and
0600, 29 November. During this period the wind was "fairly
constant" at an estimated 60 knots and the seas were from the
north northeast at 20 to 25 feet, 250 to 300 feet from crest
to crest. The vessel did take some water over the stern and
there was the normal difficulty in shiphandling to be expected with heavy following seas. After overhearing a conversation between the EDWARD Y. TOWNSEND and the DANIEL J. MORRELL
concerning the possibilities of proceeding to Thunder Bay for
shelter, the master of the BENSON FORD joined the discussion
to give information concerning the status of anchored vessels
at Thunder Bay. He reached the definite opinion that both
Captain Crawley and Captain Connelly were planning to seek
shelter at Thunder Bay. During this conversation both upbound
vessels had indicated that their speeds had been reduced.
Although the BENSON FORD was experiencing difficulty with his
AM radio due to "static electricity," he was maintaining a
continuous listening watch on channel 51 and had overheard
some communication on that channel. No actual distress communication was received on the 28 or 29th of November, however.
At 0015 29 November the BENSON FORD was at an estimated position of 055°T, 19.7 miles from Pt. Aux Barques Light. During
the period 0100 to 0130 the BENSON FORD picked up a radar
contact off her starboard beam at a distance of about 5.8
miles. At this time the BENSON FORD was on a heading of 180°.
The target was not identified but was believed to be either
the DANIEL J. MORRELL or the EDWARD Y. TOWNSEND because he
knew of no other vessels in that general area. The target was
intermittent due to weather conditions and no other target
on his starboard side was observed. The BENSON FORD suffered
no damages as a result of the storm. The master of the BEN-
SON FORD indicated that the weather conditions experienced
were more severe than expected. He had anticipated winds from
the NNW. He also expressed the opinion that he would not have
been able to safely lower his lifeboats during this storm,
had it been necessary.

33. The SS KINSMAN INDEPENDENT, a Great Lakes bulk freighter constructed in 1907, proceeded upbound into Lake Huron and passed the Lake Huron Lightship with a cargo of coal at 1727 EST on 28 November. The master, Captain Zernie Newman, stated that at that time there were light winds from the west. As the vessel approached the Harbor Beach area the wind had moved to the North and was 45 knots. The engine was held at 3/4 speed in order to maintain steerageway. This speed was 83 RPM, which would normally give the vessel a speed of approximately 10.6 MPH. At 2205 speed was reduced to 68 RPM. At 0145, 29 November 1966, when the KINSMAN INDEPENDENT was in position 010°T and 3.2 miles from Harbor Beach Light, it was blown off course and was caught in the trough of the sea for approximately four minutes before being able to reverse course to return to Port Huron. The vessel had been unable to regain its former heading. Until being blown around she had been able to hold into the sea without too much difficulty. The wind had increased to an estimated 47 to 55 knots. The draft of the KINSMAN INDEPENDENT on entering Lake Huron was 17'2" forward and 18'9" aft. The horsepower of this 592 foot vessel is 1800.

34. Captain Newman had expected the wind and seas to go to the Northwest and that his vessel would be in the lee of the eastern shore of Michigan. At the height of the storm the estimated height of the sea was 15 to 17 feet and he observed two "rollers" with an estimated height of 25 to 28 feet. Until his return to Port Huron for refuge, Captain Newman had intended to continue through the storm to Superior, Wisconsin. Captain Newman indicated that he had experienced one storm on the Great Lakes that was more severe than that experienced on 28 and 29 November. This was a 1952 storm in Lake Superior in which the winds were about 95 MPH and the seas 25 feet high.

35. Captain William L. Hull was Second Mate on the DANIEL J. MORRELL in November 1958 when that vessel was proceeding in a storm in Lake Superior. The winds at that time reached 100

miles per hour and the seas reached a height of 25 feet. The DANIEL J. MORRELL was then in ballast and additional water ballast was carried in the cargo hold.

36. The following upbound vessels were also in the general area off Pt. Aux Barques, during the storm on 28 and 29 November 1966:

a. SS HOWARD L. SHAW (Canadian)

This 451'6" vessel of 4769 gross tons, built in 1900 at Wyandotte, Michigan, passed Lake Huron Lightship at 1545, 28 November 1966. At 2115 she was abeam of Harbor Beach, proceeding at three-fourths speed and making one to two knots over the bottom. At 2330, 29 November 1966 she was blown off course, and after making two unsuccessful attempts to regain her heading into the sea, proceeded to Port Huron for refuge. The HOWARD L. SHAW was light and in ballast. She had no radio contact with the DANIEL J. MORRELL while in Lake Huron on 28 or 29 November.

b. SS FRED A. MANSKE, O.N. 206695

This is a 504 foot self-unloading Great Lakes bulk freighter, built in 1909 of 2500 horsepower. Although the vessel was almost blown around, she proceeded upbound to her destination, through the area off Pt. Aux Barques, during the storm. The master was reluctant to come about because of the topside weight of the self-unloading boom.

c. SS ROBERT HOBSON, O.N. 226175

This 586 foot Great Lakes bulk freighter, built in 1926 of 2200 horsepower, passed the Lake Huron Lightship at 1736 EST, 28 November 1966. She was blown around at 0230, 29 November 1966, approximately three to four miles above Harbor Beach, and proceeded to the Port Huron area. The ROBERT HOBSON, which was loaded with coal to the winter marks, sustained no known damages. The master of this vessel indicated that the winds experienced were not surprising but the seas were more than were anticipated under such wind conditions.

d. SS HARRY COULBY, O. N. 226742

This 615 foot Great Lakes bulk freighter, built in 1927 of 5000 horsepower, passed the Lake Huron Lightship at 0126 EST, 29 November 1966. When at a position 6 miles above Port Sanilac on the upbound track, it experienced one wave estimated to be 20 feet in height and took solid water over the bow. At this time the master was informed that conditions were more severe in the Pt. Aux Barques area and that other vessels were returning downbound in the snow storm. He then intentionally reversed course and proceeded to the Port Huron area. The master of the HARRY COULBY said that the master of the HENRY STEINBRENNER reported that it took 8 minutes for that vessel to come about. The master of the HENRY STEINBRENNER intentionally turned his vessel around and returned to Port Huron.

e. Several other vessels were reported to have been blown around, turned around voluntarily or proceeded through Lake Huron at various times during 28 and 29 November 1966.

37. The U. S. Coast Guard Cutter ACACIA (WLB-406), having departed Harbor Beach, Michigan at 1650, 28 November 1966 with a deck load consisting of two Coast Guard craft, the CG-40507 and CG-36550, while en route to Sault Ste. Marie, Michigan was diverted to assist personnel on the grounded M/V NORDMEER off Thunder Bay Island Light. At 2215 she was released from the NORDMEER assistance ease. At 2330, CG-36550 broke loose due to heavy weather. At this time the vessel was at an estimated position of 44°12'N, 82°51'W and was attempting to reach shelter at Thunder Bay. At 0300, 29 November 1966 both the CG-40507 and the CG-36550 were loose on deck and were receiving damages. The seas were estimated to be 15 to 25 feet in height. The wind was reported as 40 to 50 knots. The ACACIA then came about at an estimated position of 44°30'N, 82°55'W to head for shelter. She was unable to enter Harbor Beach because of the heavy seas and accordingly proceeded to Port Huron, Michigan, for safe refuge.

38. While the DANIEL J. MORRELL was taking on fuel at Windsor, Ontario on the morning of 28 November 1966, Dennis N. Hale boarded the vessel and assumed his regular duties as watchman. Hale had a total of three years sea service, all of which was served on board the DANIEL J. MORRELL. He had been serving as watchman for approximately a year.

39. Hale normally stood the 4-8 watch and commenced his last watch shortly after the vessel passed the Lake Huron Lightship at approximately 1530, 28 November 1966. Between 1600 and 1630, Hale, as directed, entered the cargo holds for the purpose of marking leaks and cargo bucket damages, which were incurred during normal unloading operations in way of side tank slopes. Damage to side tank slopes had been repaired several times during the 1966 operating season. The vessel's smooth log indicated that the last repairs in that area had been completed in Buffalo, N. Y. on 26 October 1966. He marked three leaks, one in the general area of number 6 hatch and two in the general area of number 8 hatch. He was unable to drive wedges into the holes because the cracks were not parted sufficiently to receive wedges. The largest of the cracks was described as "moon shaped" and 8 inches long. The three cracks were "spurting water." He was unable to enter the number three cargo hold because free surface water extended from the after bulkhead of number three cargo hold to midway into number two. He estimated the depth of water to be 18 inches at the after bulkhead of #3 cargo hold. Hale attributed the water to leaks from the side tanks and so informed the master of the amount of water in the cargo holds. The vessel's hatch covers were in place and tarpaulins were on deck, rolled up adjacent to the hatches. At 2000, 28 November, at the time of completing his watch, Hale indicated that it was snowing but the weather was not severe, and the vessel was riding "well." He was able to proceed aft to the galley for food after getting off watch. However, at the time of his going to bed at about 2130, the weather was worsening. Hale's quarters were located on the spar deck, starboard side forward, adjacent to the anchor windlass room. At the time of

going to bed he could hear the anchors bumping against the bow. Other than the noise produced by the anchors, Hale was not aware of the actual weather and sea conditions from the time of going to bed until at or about 0200, 29 November 1966. At about that time he was awakened by what was described as a loud bang. A few minutes later he heard another bang. At this time, books from his book shelf fell out into the deck. The book shelf had no retaining bar and was installed in a fore and aft direction. He became alarmed and decided to get up. He then learned that his bunk light was inoperative. About this time the general alarm was sounded. He jumped up, grabbed his lifejacket and ran out into the starboard passageway. There were no lights on in the forward section of the vessel, but as he looked aft he could see lights on the after superstructure. He noticed that the center of the vessel was "higher" than the after part of the vessel; that is to say, it was in a hogging condition. He went back into his room to look for his pants, but in the darkness and excitement he could find only his peacoat. He then proceeded to the forward liferaft. There was melting snow on the deck. He had looked for the lifeboats but was convinced that they both had already been lowered. While still forward he could hear what he took to be metal cracking and working or rubbing together. When he reached the forward liferaft, there were several men standing around it. He thought the whole forward or deck crew was there at that time. No attempt was made to proceed to the lifeboat area because of the damage in the midship section. Someone said, "get on the raft and hold on tight." He indicated that virtually all deck force personnel, including the Master, 1st Mate and 2nd Mate sat on the raft to await the sinking of the vessel. No attempt was made to throw the raft over the side and no instructions regarding the use of lifesaving equipment were given by any of the ship's officers in Hale's presence. One crew member tried to get men off the raft in order to open the storage locker to reach the distress flares. The master decided to wait until the raft was in the water to use the flares. The crew members assembled at the raft were in various stages of dress, some with various items of clothing missing. For example, Hale was wearing only a pair of shorts, lifejacket and peacoat. They were all wearing lifejackets. Hale knew that there were two vessels following fairly close behind the DANIEL J. MORRELL earlier and Captain Crawley had indicated that there had been a vessel sighted off the port bow. Hale did not actually see any other vessels immediately prior to or at any time after the sinking. Two men had attempted to tie themselves to the raft with line. Hale saw only one person on the after end of the ship, but he could not be certain of his identity. Although there were no lights in the midship area, Hale indicated he did observe that the crack in the vessel started in the area of the gunwale bar, starboard side, in the general area of hatches 11 and 12, and proceed across to the port side. The forward section's deck at the starboard side seemed to drop lower than the after section in a twisting effect. Hale could see metal sparks as the two sections of the vessel rubbed together. He could also see steam coming from the parted steam line. Then the vessel broke into two sections and the stern section appeared to be pushing and ramming the forward section. This, together with sea and wind action, caused the bow section to work around to port, reaching a perpendicular angle in relation to the stern section. (See Exhibit No. 49.) The stern section appeared to be still under power and continued to bump into the port side of the bow section. As the bow section swung to port and parted from the after section, it started settling and very shortly thereafter the forward life raft and several members of the crew were washed over the starboard side. Time elapse from the sounding of the emergency alarm until the vessel parted was estimated to be eight minutes. The raft was thrown well clear of both sections of the vessel and no one remained on the raft as it entered the water. Hale came up within approximately 10 feet of the raft. By the time he reached the raft, two deckhands, Arthur E. Stojek and John J. Cleary, Jr., had already arrived. Then Charles Fosbender, wheelsman, reached the raft and they were all able to crawl onto the raft. Hale saw no one in the water prior to his going over

the side. After his entry into the water, the only persons he
saw were the other three on the raft and one person still on
the forecastle of the vessel. He never saw a lifeboat or the
after raft in the water. Hale was of the opinion when the
forward raft entered the water that the after raft was still
on the vessel. None of the four men on the raft were on watch
at the time of the casualty. No one indicated to Hale any
knowledge as to the cause of the casualty, incidents leading
up to the actual sinking or whether radio distress signals
had been transmitted. Hale heard the master state on 28
November that channel 52 was inoperative. There were no other
known radio problems on board the DANIEL J. MORRELL. The
vessel's speed or heading, and the direction of the wind and
sea in relation to the vessel at the time of the casualty is
unknown. He did not know the vessel's location at the time of
sinking. Approximately 15 minutes after Hale entered the
water he observed the after portion of the bow section settle
evenly beneath the water, followed by the stem. The raft was
at a distance of approximately 200 yards from the bow section
and an estimated one-half to one mile from the stern section
when the bow sank. The stern still seemed to be under power
and lights were still visible. The men on the raft did not
see the stern section sink. Other than the actual breaking up
of the vessel, no fires, explosions or any other material,
machinery or equipment casualties were observed by Hale while
on board or after going over the side. The life raft was
provided with the equipment required by Federal Regulations.
Hale used several of the distress flares within a short
period after sinking as there were other vessels known to be
in the general area. Two flares were lost over the side.
After having fired the signal pistol two or three times, the
handle and barrel separated into two pieces. He was able to
hold them together in order to fire off the remaining parachute flares. Hale knew of no other deficiencies with lifesaving equipment. All the parachute flares and hand held
flares were used within the first 24 hours. The storage
locker and other portions of the wood and metal raft structure sustained damages as it went over the side. However, it

remained intact and offered adequate support for the four men. The men lay on the raft huddled together on one end, there being no other means of keeping warm. Hale testified that Cleary and Stojek died around 0600, 29 November 1966 and that Fosbender died around 1600 the same day. They were all believed to be conscious until shortly before death. The cause of death for these three men was listed on their Death Certificates as drowning. Exposure was listed as an antecedent cause. The life raft supporting Hale and the three deceased men was located by the Coast Guard at 1600, 30 November 1966. Hale was semi-conscious when he was taken from the raft. He was able to give preliminary testimony to Coast Guard Investigating Officers on 1 December 1966. (See Exhibit 26.) He suffered from exposure, frost bite of his feet and right hand and sustained other minor injuries. As a result, he is still incapacitated.

40. Hale testified during the preliminary interrogation that prior to the sinking, the vessel was "sound" as far as he was concerned. However, he stated that there were some rivets marked for replacement by Frank Brian, wheelsman, throughout the cargo holds just before winter lay up in 1965. He could give no estimate as to the number of marked rivets. He indicated that he didn't know if any had been replaced but that he knew some still had not been replaced prior to the 1966 season. These rivets were alleged to be in the shell plating between the side tank tops and the spar deck. At initial questioning, he knew of no other structural discrepancies. When questioned before the Marine Board, he testified that over 1000 rivets were marked for replacement in the shell plating between the main and spar decks, port and starboard, and that these rivets had not been replaced at the time of the casualty. He related that about a week prior to the latter questioning, Harvey F. Hays, deck watchman on board the DANIEL J. MORRELL in 1965, told him that one-fourth of the shell rivets in the side tanks were bad. Neither the company representatives, inspectors, surveyors, or previous vessel personnel who were questioned had ever seen or heard of

defective or marked rivets in the shell plating between the
main and spar decks.

41. Hays testified that the 1st mate had given Frank Brian
instructions in mid-November 1965, in his presence, for Brian
and Hays to enter No. 4 and 5 port tanks to mark leaky rivets with paint. He stated that Brian was in charge as he had
30 years experience. Hays stated that he observed two leaking
bead welds in the area of lapped butt plates. He indicated that the worst leak was approximately seven inches in a
vertical direction. He also stated that there were 250 to 500
leaky shell rivets marked in these two tanks from above the
turn of the bilge to within two feet of the side tank tops
and that the vessel's side plating was partially wet when the
leaky rivets were marked. He saw no sheared or missing rivets. The leaky rivets were allegedly grouped to the extent
that the men painted circles around some areas up to 3 and 4
feet in diameter. A report of the condition of the rivets was
reportedly made to the 1st mate by Brian. Hays also entered
the cargo holds to mark up bucket damage for repair during
winter lay up.

42. Hays stated that several of the vessel's side tanks were
leaking during the 1965 season and that as a result of his
personally sounding vessel tanks, he had observed the collection of up to 3 inches in a side tank within a 24 hour period. He personally observed up to seven inches in side tanks
and on one occasion up to 10 inches that he attributed to
leakage. The port side tanks 4 and 5 were leaking more than
the others.

43. Hays testified that he had never discussed the structural
condition of the DANIEL J. MORRELL with Dennis Hale. Hays' total sea experience consists of service on the DANIEL J. MORRELL
from 3 June to 21 December 1965 as deckhand and deck watch.

44. Mr. Frank Brian informed the Board that he has never entered side and double bottom tanks to mark leaky rivets. He
considered this work to be the mate's responsibility. He did

enter all the DANIEL J. MORRELL's port side and double bottom tanks in the Spring of 1965 to remove debris left by shipyard personnel. On this occasion he saw no structural defects.

45. After being informed by an official of the Bethlehem Steel Corporation at 1215 EST, 30 November 1966 that the DANIEL J. MORRELL was overdue, the U. S. Coast Guard Rescue Coordination Center, Cleveland, Ohio initiated an all ships broadcast, requesting that all vessels be on the lookout for that vessel. A fixed wing aircraft, CG-1266, en route from Alpena, Michigan to Detroit, Michigan was directed to offload cargo at Detroit and then commence a search for the DANIEL J. MORRELL. At 1312, 30 November 1966 the Coast Guard in Cleveland, Ohio was informed that the SS G. G. POST had sighted a body wearing a life jacket stencilled with the name, "DANIEL J. MORRELL", 8 miles, 005° true from the Harbor Beach Breakwater Light. The CG-30386 had already been dispatched by the Harbor Beach Coast Guard Station and actually recovered the body at 1210, 30 November 1966. The Coast Guard aircraft, CG-1266, arrived in the general area of the disaster at 1335 and was designated as on scene commander. The following Coast Guard units participated in the search:

Vessels and small craft

USCGC MACKINAW (WAGB-83)
USCGC BRAMBLE (WLB-392)
USCGC ACACIA (WLB-406)
CG-30386 and CG-36463 from Harbor Beach Coast Guard
                          Station
CG-40560 from the Port Huron Coast Guard Station
CG-40558 from the Saginaw River Coast Guard Station

Aircraft

Helicopters CG-1395 and CG-1412 and fixed wing air-
                    craft CG-1242 and CG-1266 from CG Air
                    Station, Traverse City, Michigan

Helicopters CG-1401 and CG-1415 from CG Air Station,
Detroit, Michigan

Upon arrival of the CGC MACKINAW in the area of the casualty, she was designated as on scene commander.

46. In addition to the first body recovered at 1210, 30 November 1966 by CG-30386, additional bodies, the survivor and debris were recovered as follows:

a. At or about 1600, 30 November 1966, seven bodies were recovered by CG-30386 and helicopters CG-1401 and CG-1415, within a five mile radius of a position seven miles, 025° true from Harbor Beach Breakwater Light.

b. At about 1600, 30 November 1966, three bodies and one survivor were recovered from the DANIEL J. MORRELL's forward life raft, on the beach, three miles below Huron City, Michigan by helicopter CG-1395. The survivor, Dennis Hale, was transported by the helicopter to the Harbor Beach General Hospital.

c. At about 0930, 1 December 1966, one body was recovered ten and one-half miles, 137° true from the Harbor Beach Breakwater Light by the CGC MACKINAW.

d. At about 0945, 1 December 1966, at a position of 43°40'N, 82°20.5'W, two bodies were recovered by the CGC ACACIA.

e. At about 1355, on 1 December 1966, at a position of 43°37'N, 82°20'W, six bodies were recovered by the CGC ACACIA.

f. At about 1445, 5 December 1966, one body was recovered under the DANIEL J. MORRELL's after liferaft at Pt. Aux Barques by a commercial salvager. The raft was generally in good condition, with only minor damages.

g. On the morning of 11 December 1966, one body was re-covered by the Ontario Provincial Police on the beach eight miles north of Kincardine, Ontario.

The active search continued until 1905 EST, 4 December 1966. Daily surveillance searches were conducted along the shoreline several days thereafter, as weather permitted, in attempts to locate the remaining bodies and vessel debris.

47. In addition to a number of Great Lakes vessels there were several Coast Guard units in the Lake Huron area that were maintaining continuous listening watches on channel 51 (2182 kc.) at the time of the casualty. No distress message was received from the DANIEL J. MORRELL by Coast Guard units or other vessels in the area. The material and debris from the DANIEL J. MORRELL recovered and collected during and after completion of the active search including two liferafts, several life jackets, life rings, boat oars, etc., as indicated in Exhibit 52, have been released to the vessel owners.

48. During November and December 1960, while the DANIEL J. MORRELL was on dry-dock in Ashtabula, Ohio approximately 9500 shell rivets and 13 shell plates were replaced. Numer-ous replacements and repairs were completed to internals in way thereof. Various other repairs were also completed at this time. (See Exhibit No. 21.) All the above repairs were allegedly required as result of the vessel surging against the dock at Taconite Harbor, Minnesota on 2 December 1959; heavy weather on 18 November 1958 in Lake Superior; rubbing of the bottom in Nicolet Lake on 3 August 1958; the vessel's striking of a dock prior to 26 June 1960 at an undetermined time and place; the vessel's striking of a wall at Lock 4, St. Mary's River, Sault Ste. Marie, Michigan, on 15 June 1960; and as a result of cargo loading and unloading "buck-et" damages prior to the date of drydocking. It is noted that bucket damage repairs included cropping and renewing sections of auxiliary deck stringer plates at some hatches. One 8" by 24" section of the inboard edge of the auxiliary deck string-er at hatch number 11 starboard side was cropped and renewed

by welding. All repairs during the drydocking of the DANIEL J. MORRELL in November and December 1960, were completed and tested satisfactorily.

49. The subject vessel was next drydocked in Toledo, Ohio, on 18 February 1966 and was given credit for drydocking by the U. S. Coast Guard on 25 February 1966. From drydocking in December 1960 to drydocking in February 1966, there were no reported major damages to the DANIEL J. MORRELL and no major repairs or alterations were completed to the vessel during that period. However, there were minor repairs completed during this period, such as routine "bucket damage" repairs in way of cargo holds.

50. Seven (7) inspectors and surveyors participated in the 1966 drydock inspection of subject vessel. This group included the Fleet Engineer of the Bethlehem Steel Corporation and his assistant, a representative of U. S. Salvage, a representative of the American Bureau of Shipping and three Coast Guard inspectors, including one boiler and two hull inspectors. During this inspection, the entire external body, all side and double bottom tanks, forepeak and after peak tanks and all other vessel compartments were inspected thoroughly. As a result of this inspection, three shell plates in the starboard "E" strake were removed and replaced by two longer plates. The plates removed were E-21-S, E-22-S and E-23-S, located between frames 107-127. The plates were installed with welded butts and riveted seams whereas the previous installation consisted of riveted butts and seams. In addition, eleven (11) bilge brackets and three (3) web floors in the area involved were cropped back and replaced or partially replaced because of buckling. These repairs were necessitated by damages sustained at an undetermined date and discovered during the 1966 drydock inspection. The three (3) plates were set in approximately two inches. The remainder of the hull plating appeared to be in good condition. There was no condition found during the dry-dock examination to indicate the necessity for drilling or gauging to determine the thickness

of metal. While the vessel was on drydock, approximately 50 shell rivets were replaced as required by the inspection party. In eight (8) of the vessel's side and double bottom tanks, the Coast Guard inspector required numerous minor or routine type repairs, such as the refastening of stiffeners and brackets and repairing cracked welds in brackets, stiffeners, and angles. In the number 4 starboard double bottom tank the Coast Guard inspector required that a seven (7) foot by one and one-half (1.5) foot section of the after watertight bulkhead be cropped and replaced, necessitated by a fracture in the bulkhead plate adjacent to the bottom transverse standing angle. Numerous repairs were completed in cargo holds. These were necessitated by bucket damage. The senior Coast Guard hull inspector present during the drydock inspection made the following entry in the Drydock Examination Book for February 1966: "It was noted that approximately 80% of the bottom keelson shell rivets had been renewed recently, probably at the last credit drydocking. Deterioration seems to be effecting these rivets more than other bottom rivets. Although it does not present a problem at this time, they may well require renewal at the next drydock exam." He considered that the amount of deterioration was not sufficient to justify the issuing of a requirement to replace the rivets. This entry was made in the Drydock Examination Book for future reference only. Neither of the Coast Guard hull inspectors could determine the reason for the "unusual" deterioration, but did postulate that electrolytic action was involved. All repairs that were required by Coast Guard inspectors or other members of the inspection party were completed satisfactorily and were inspected by Coast Guard inspectors after completion. Upon completion of the drydock examination, all drydock inspection items were checked off in the Drydock Examination Book as having been completed and the senior hull inspector and the boiler inspector signed the entry: "In my opinion the vessel is fit for the service and route specified." There were no outstanding requirements upon completion of the dry-dock examination of the DANIEL J. MORRELL. All inspectors and surveyors interrogated indicated that at the conclusion of the drydock inspection, this vessel was in good condition.

51. The last annual inspection was completed 15 April 1966 at the Lakefront Ore Dock, Toledo, Ohio. All items required to be inspected by Federal Regulation were examined and were determined to be in satisfactory condition at the comple- tion of the annual inspection. The Load Line Certificate was endorsed by an American Bureau of Shipping Surveyor, on 26 February 1966. Fire and boat drills were conducted at annual inspection and at the time of mid-season inspection at Buffa- lo, New York, 20 July 1966. During the annual inspection, all personnel except the master, the mate and the chief engineer were exercised in the starboard lifeboat. The port life- boat was swung out. Crew performance during the boat drill was considered to be fair because crew members were slow in launching the boat. The first mate then instructed the crew as to their duties. The performance of the second and third boat crews was much improved. The fire and boat drills during the mid-season inspection were conducted satisfactorily. There were no requirements outstanding against the vessel or its equipment at the time of completion of the annual or mid-season inspections. Subsequent to the date of completion of annual inspection and prior to the date of the casualty there were no known hull or structural damages suffered by the vessel.

52. Prior to winter lay up of the DANIEL J. MORRELL in De- cember 1965, a winter work list was prepared for that vessel and was signed by the master for deck items and by the chief engineer for engineering items. The deck section of the work list was prepared by the 1st mate. Of the 46 items on the winter work list all were completed except two which were not of structural significance. The deck section of the work list contained the following item, "Leaks in the hull will be marked. Port tanks make water." No other item pertaining to midship structural strength of the vessel was contained on the list. The master and chief engineer serving on board

subject vessel at the time of winter lay up in 1965 both
testified that no other vessel deficiencies were reported by
crew members prior to winter lay up. Captain Hull served as
master of the DANIEL J. MORRELL from July 1964 until 3 August
1966, when he was relieved by Captain Crawley. Captain Hull
stated that the side tanks and cargo holds of the MORRELL
were entered by vessel personnel for the purpose of marking leaky rivets in the shell plating and bucket damage in
the cargo holds and to inspect for other damage in the Fall
of 1965. He estimated that a maximum of twelve (12) leaking rivets were reported in the shell plating in way of side
tanks, although he could not remember which side tanks were
involved. He indicated that the reason the side tanks were
entered for checking rivets was that some of the side tanks
were "making water." He said that maximum leakage into any
side tank was approximately 5 to 6 inches over a period of a
three or four day trip. He did not report the leaks to the
vessel owners nor did he direct personnel to enter the tanks
until shortly prior to winter lay up because he did not consider the leakage to be significant or excessive.

53. Captain Hull considered that the leaking shell rivets had
been corrected during drydocking. However, during the 1966
season there were two or possibly three unidentified side
tanks that leaked slightly. He did not inform the company of
this condition.

54. The fire and sanitary piping to the forward part of the
vessel was installed through the port side tanks. Leaking
joints in this piping necessitated repairs during the 1966
season and the vessel operators had planned to relocate these
pipes on the spar deck during winter lay up in 1966-1967. The
fire line was also used for washdown. This same situation has
existed in the past on other vessels of the Bethlehem Fleet
and similar corrective measures have been taken. Upon departing the DANIEL J. MORRELL on 3 August 1966, Captain Hull knew
of nothing that would cast doubt as to the soundness of that
vessel. He had received no report or complaints from vessel

personnel and made no report to company officials to indicate any outstanding vessel structural, equipment or mechanical deficiencies through that date.

55. A Coast Guard inspector boarded the EDWARD Y. TOWNSEND at Sault Ste. Marie, Ontario on 2 December 1966, to conduct a heavy weather damage survey. The following conditions were found:

a. The visual part of the crack on the spar deck was approximately 13 inches in length with a maximum opening of approximately 1/8 inch. The crack was almost perpendicular to the axis of the vessel. There was a herringbone effect giving the indication that the crack commenced somewhere beneath the number 10 hatch coaming's forward supporting standing angle at the starboard corner.

b. At the forward starboard corner of number 10 and number 11 hatches, rivets in the deck strap showed signs of working. There were no signs of working on the spar deck, port side. Visual inspection of the shell plating, sheer strake and gunnel bars, port and starboard, revealed no apparent change in form resulting from stress.

c. In numbers 3, 4 and 5 doublebottom and side tanks, starboard, there was minor distortion of metal adjacent to some side keelson lightening holes and there was evidence of previous minor stress corrosion. At some of the distortions there was evidence of working. It could not be determined whether the minor distortion was the result of recent working or was previously existing, but there was indication that rust and scale had recently been jarred or popped loose from some of the stress corrosion areas. There was only one crack noticed in way of the stress corrosion. This was a crack approximately six inches in length commencing diagonally from the edge of a lightening hole. This crack was not a new one as scale or rust had formed over the edges. There were several rivets in the center vertical keel that showed signs of recent working. There was an old crack of approximately 6 feet

in length in the after bulkhead of number 4 starboard double
bottom tank between the outboard side keelson and the turn of
the bilge. This crack was in the same general location as one
discovered on the DANIEL J. MORRELL in February 1966. Some
of the shell rivets at the bulkhead standing angle in this
area were loose, leaked slightly and showed signs of deterioration. It could not be determined whether the bulkhead had
worked recently but there was no apparent distortion. The
distortion, stress corrosion and evidence of working rivets
were more pronounced in the number 4 side and double bottom
tanks than in adjacent areas. The corresponding tanks on the
port side showed some signs of minor distortion at the lightening holes of the side keelsons.

d. The metal in the midship area of the vessel, including
deck, shell, internals and all structural members appeared to
be in surprisingly good material condition. The weardown, or
deterioration, was considered negligible.

e. Other than the normal stress corrosion, cracks and evidence of working rivets as indicated above, there was nothing found that would explain the reason for the crack in the
spar deck. Excluding the crack in the spar deck, no evidence
of major structural weakness was found.

f. The EDWARD Y. TOWNSEND's Certificate of Inspection
was withdrawn as a result of this inspection and requirement
was issued directing the vessel to be drydocked for further
internal and external inspection and necessary repairs. A
Permit to Proceed to the location of a drydock was issued,
authorizing the vessel to be towed unmanned.

g. The owners of the EDWARD Y. TOWNSEND have agreed to
provide samples of metal removed in way of the crack for
analysis at such time as repair work is commenced. At present, the vessel is in a winter lay up status at Sault Ste.
Marie, Ontario.

56. From initial construction through the date of Subject
casualty, the SS DANIEL J. MORRELL and the SS EDWARD Y.

TOWNSEND had no significant structural or propulsion unit changes or alterations that would alter their classification as sister ships. The latter vessel was reboilered in 1946 and repowered with a Skinner Unaflow engine in 1954.

57. The Bethlehem Steel Corporation contracted the McQueen Marine Company, Amherstburg, Ontario, Canada to locate and positively identify the sunken DANIEL J. MORRELL. Due to adverse weather conditions experienced while attempting to locate the MORRELL between 13 December 1966 and 20 December 1966, attempts to locate and identify that vessel were abandoned on the latter date.

58. The Commandant, U. S. Coast Guard contracted with Ocean Systems Incorporated, Alexandria, Virginia through the cooperation of the Supervisor of Salvage, U. S. Navy, to locate, identify, take television pictures of vessel structure and retrieve metal samples from the DANIEL J. MORRELL. The U. S. Coast Guard Cutter BRAMBLE (WLB-392) was used as a working platform for the entire survey operations. On 6 January 1967, after mooring over a target located by magnetic detection equipped aircraft from the U. S. Naval Air Station, Grosse Ile, Michigan, divers working from the BRAMBLE were able to positively identify by television pictures the stern section of the DANIEL J. MORRELL. Further diving operations were then continued from 14 January 1967 to 2 February 1967.

59. As a result of the diving operations, the following facts were established:

   a. The stern section of the vessel was resting on the bottom of Lake Huron in approximately 200 to 210 feet of water on a heading of about 320° true. It has settled appreciably in the mud, and has a slight port list. She has a slight trim by the forward end. There were piles of mud on the spar deck adjacent to the point of the crack and it appeared that the forward end had plowed into the bottom first. This area of the stern was buried in mud to within 6' to 7' of the spar deck.

b. The primary crack in the deck and sheerstrake on the starboard side occurred at web frame 107. This frame is located adjacent to and even with the forward coaming of number 11 hatch. The fracture line on the deck, starboard, ran through a transverse row of rivet holes to the hatch coaming. The forward portion of the number 11 hatch coaming was missing. The crack in the starboard sheerstrake was basically vertical and passed from rivet hole to rivet hole. The location of the break on the port side was between hatches 11 and 12 at about frame 113. The break in the deck stringer followed a transverse row of rivets. The crack in the sheerstrake, port side, was vertical and did not occur in the area of rivets. The port deck seam strap cracked through a line of rivets about six inches forward of the break in the deck stringer. All underdeck longitudinals in the area of the break were bent, twisted, torn loose and displaced from their normal positions. Remaining deck and side plating as well as longitudinals show evidence of severe distortions. Some longitudinals were doubled back upon themselves. Deck and side plating showed evidence of extreme bending. Some sections had been bent back upon themselves to approximately 180° from original. The deck stringer starboard side had been bent down to an angle of about 90 degrees. A section of this plate was recovered for analysis. The surface of the crack in this plate contains chevrons pointing inboard. A large section of the sheerstrake starboard with a section of the seam strap and "L" strake attached was also recovered. Chevrons on the edge of fractured surface on either side of the 3rd rivet hole below the upper edge of the sheerstrake pointed toward that rivet hole. This section of side metal had been bent outboard and around upon itself to 180° from normal. The retrieved metal shows signs of little or no wear down or deterioration and the rivets contained therein were in very good condition. The edges of rivet holes showed no signs of wastage. The forward edges of the retrieved metal were shiny and flattened as if they had sustained severe pounding by other metal.

c. Cargo hatches and the coal bunker were found open. Hatch covers were strewn about the area of the hulk. Many hatch clamps had been broken.

d. The port and starboard lifeboat davits were found in the cranked-in position. The port lifeboat was missing and has not been recovered. The starboard lifeboat was hanging over the starboard side still attached to the after boat falls. Its boat cover was in place. The after mast had toppled and had fallen in the area of the missing port lifeboat.

e. None of the missing crew members of the DANIEL J. MORRELL were located as a result of the diving operations.

f. The forward section of the DANIEL J. MORRELL was not located.

g. Diving operations were hampered by silt, weather and sea conditions and the divers were not able to make an internal survey to determine distortions or weaknesses that might have contributed to the casualty.

60. The report of the metallurgical study, dated 6 March 1967, of steel plate samples from the DANIEL J. MORRELL and completed by the Battelle Memorial Institute, Columbus Laboratories, Columbus, Ohio supports the following facts:

a. A brittle fracture typical of many prior ship fractures in pre-1948 steel occurred in the spar deck and sheer strake on the starboard side at frame 107.

b. The source of the fracture in the deck plate was not contained in the sample recovered from the hulk. However, the chevron pattern in the fracture indicated that the fracture initiated inboard of the sample retrieved.

c. The fracture in the sheer strake at frame 107 initiated at the 3rd rivet hole below the upper edge of the sheer strake.

d. The original weight of the deck and sheer strake was 40 pounds per square foot (assumed to be 39.98 pounds rather than 40.8 pounds). This corresponds to a thickness of .980 inches. The average thickness of the sample retrieved was .965 inches, which would indicate corrosion of less than 2 per cent.

e. The chemical and physical properties and microstructure of the steel were typical of ship plate steel used prior to 1948. The nil ductility temperature as determined by "The Standard Method for Naval Research Laboratory Drop Weight Test" was 50°F. The 15 foot pound "V" notch Charpy transition temperature averaged 97°F.

61. Of the 22 persons recovered, 13 drowned and 9 died of exposure.

62. The Federal Bureau of Investigation has given authority to include their reports showing positive identification of the persons recovered into the record.

CONCLUSIONS

Based on the foregoing Findings of Fact, it is concluded that:

1. The casualty was caused by a structural failure in the hull girder amidships which resulted in the break-up of the vessel, and subsequent sinking with loss of life.

2. The cause of the structural failure was a combination of factors which produced successive brittle fractures. These factors were:

a. High load due to extremely heavy weather conditions.

b. A notch sensitive steel.

c. A notch. Among others, some of the possible locations of the notch are:

(1) A radial crack in a rivet hole.

(2) A welded plate insert on the inboard edge of the auxiliary stringer at number 11 hatch, starboard side.

(3) Recently incurred bucket damage to the inboard edge of the auxiliary stringer in the vicinity of frame 107, starboard side.

    d. Temperature of 33°F, which was below the nil ductility temperature of the steel.

3. The exact location of the initiation of the fracture (whether bottom, deck or side shell) is unknown. However, the most probable location was on the spar deck starboard side at frame 107 in way of the number 11 hatch corner.

4. A number of other factors, including one or any combination of the following, might have contributed to this casualty:

    a. The free surface water in cargo holds 2 and 3 might have caused an unusual strain to an already weakened area as a result of the dynamic forces of shifting weight due to pitching, rolling, pounding, and possible twisting of the vessel as its bow was blown around.

    b. The vessel might have broached and sustained the crack while attempting to hold into the sea as she was broaching or while attempting to regain her heading into the sea. It is concluded that any ballasted vessel of a design similar to that of the DANIEL J. MORRELL would suffer severe stresses and strains in sea and wind conditions such as those present on 29 November should it remain in or at angles to the trough for any length of time. This evaluation is predicated upon the fact that a 600 foot vessel at an angle of approximately 30 degrees to seas having crests of 250 to 300 feet apart will suffer severe hogging, sagging and twisting stresses.

c. The crack in the midship section occurred at Frame 107. The welded butt joining plates E-20 and E-21 was located on the starboard side also at Frame 107. Although there is no evidence to indicate any defect in this weld, the possibility exists that the butt weld contained an undetected defect at installation.

d. The crack in the after bulkhead of the number 4 starboard double bottom tank was very similar in dimension and location to the crack found on the EDWARD Y. TOWNSEND during the heavy weather damage survey conducted on 2 December 1966. Although this may be coincidence, it may tend to indicate the existence of a pattern of structural weakness on the starboard side of these two practically identical sister vessels and possibly other vessels of approximately the same age and of similar design. This is supported by the facts that the crack commenced on the EDWARD Y. TOWNSEND and the DANIEL J. MORRELL in the same general deck area, both vessels were headed into the wind and sea under the same weather and sea conditions, both vessels were light and in ballast and both probably had basically the same free surface water in their cargo holds.

5. The actual drafts, extent of ballasting, exact courses and speeds, and reaction to sea and wind conditions on board the DANIEL J. MORRELL from the time of entering Lake Huron until immediately prior to sinking, could not be determined. However, it is assumed that they were basically the same as those that existed on the EDWARD Y. TOWNSEND during the same period.

6. Although the vessel sailed from Buffalo short of the crew required by the Certificate of Inspection, the shortages were in required ratings only. The actual number of persons aboard exceeded the number required. There was no evidence of violation of law on the part of the master or company officials in this regard. There is no evidence to indicate the crew shortage contributed to the cause of the casualty.

7. The lifesaving equipment on board met the requirements of the Federal Regulations and there is no evidence to indicate that any person lost his life due to faulty or improperly maintained lifesaving equipment. However, under the circumstances that existed at the time of sinking, the lifeboats and liferafts aboard could not be used properly to save lives. Under the existing sea conditions, the lifeboats could not have been lowered and launched successfully. Notice is taken of the fact that when Great Lakes freight vessels break in two, it is probable that approximately one-half of the crew would be at the forward end and unable to move to the after end where the larger percentage of life-saving equipment is located. Had the boats been lowered safely, there would have been little hope for survival of persons aboard for an extended period since there was no means of protection from exposure. The common boat hooks in use are considered to be adequate only in calm water operation. The liferafts proved to be substantially constructed since one of the rafts showed signs of much abuse incident to the sinking and still provided adequate support. Even though these rafts were intended to float free, it could not be established why the forward raft was not thrown over the side prior to sinking. It may have been that the vessel broke up in less time than estimated by the survivor and that the master might have considered, in light of the slush on deck, the angle of the deck after the rupture, the time available, and the weight of the raft, that to wait for the vessel to sink was the safest, or only available procedure. Once in the water, the rafts offered no protection against the elements. It could not be established how and when the after raft went into the water. Had there been approved inflatable life rafts forward and aft, they probably could have been launched by vessel personnel and would have offered some protection from exposure.

8. The six persons listed as missing are presumed dead.

9. The electric cables leading forward from the source of power parted in the midships area as a result of the

commencement of the crack in that area and prior to the
sounding of the general alarm. The steam line, the general
alarm cable and all other means of communication between the
pilot house and the engineroom were also parted at about the
same time. After this, there was no source of power forward
except batteries for the general alarm.

10. The radio installation on board the DANIEL J. MORRELL
met the requirements of the applicable Federal Regulations.
The system proved to be inadequate under the existing circumstances. Power was lost forward before bridge personnel
were aware of the extreme condition that existed amidship.
Great Lakes vessels are not required to carry emergency radios. Therefore no means for transmitting a distress signal
was available after the cables were severed. More lives might
have been saved if a distress signal had been transmitted.
Although it was known that problems existed in the use of
channel 52 prior to the sinking, a distress message probably
could have been transmitted had there been a source of power
forward. There was no evidence of any difficulty in reception
on any other radio frequency on the DANIEL J. MORRELL.

11. The free surface water sighted by Hale in the cargo holds
resulted from side tank slope damage. It is apparent that
Hale would not have been directed to enter the holds for
marking leaks in the side tank slopes and driving wedges into
the cracks if ballast had previously been pumped in intentionally. It could not be determined whether this water was
pumped from the cargo holds subsequent to its discovery by
Hale in the afternoon. The tonnage of free surface water in
the cargo holds could not be accurately determined since the
vessel drafts are not known. In lieu of the estimated 18"
there might have been nearer 45" of water at the after bulkhead of No. 3 cargo hold, as was the situation on the EDWARD Y.
TOWNSEND. It is noted that water extended to approximately
the center of No. 2 cargo hold on both vessels when discovered. It is estimated that the quantity of water in the cargo
holds could have been from 300 to 800 tons. The effect of

this quantity of water is not considered to have significantly changed the vessel's stability, which was more than adequate even with the reduction of the metacentric height caused by the free surface water. There was no evidence to indicate water was intentionally pumped into the vessel's cargo holds during this last trip.

12. The signal pistol came apart probably because the screw type hinge pin located forward of the trigger assembly and connecting the barrel of the pistol to the handle was either jarred loose or worked loose in use.

13. It is concluded that the inspections conducted by the Coast Guard during the 1966 drydocking, annual and midseason inspections were conducted in accordance with the Federal Regulations and in keeping with Coast Guard standards. There were no known deficiencies concerning the vessel's structure, equipment or machinery at the time of completion of these inspections.

14. The operators of the DANIEL J. MORRELL had not been informed of leaking rivets or any major structural, machinery or equipment deficiencies from the beginning of the 1966 season until the time of sinking. They were aware of minor items that had been repaired periodically, e. g., bucket damage to side tank slopes, radio deficiencies and leaking sanitary and fire main piping.

15. Other than the leaking shell rivets, which allowed leakage into the side tanks, leaking side tank slopes — which is common aboard Great Lakes bulk (non self-unloading) freighters — , and the non-use of tarpaulins or equivalent means for insuring tightness of the hatches there was no evidence to indicate that vessel watertight integrity was not being properly maintained.

16. There was evidence of violation of 46 CFR 97.15-20 in that although the hatch covers were in place, tarpaulins, gaskets or similar devices were not used to ensure

watertightness of the hatches prior to entering Lake Huron on 28 November 1966 in the face of adverse weather. However, there is no evidence that this violation either caused or contributed to the cause of the casualty. There is evidence that other vessels are proceeding during Fall and Spring months while in a ballasted condition without ensuring watertightness of the cargo hatch covers. There is evidence that it is common practice to install tarpaulins over sliding steel type hatch covers only when the vessel is loaded, regardless of weather conditions. Other than the evidence of violation of 46 CFR 97.15-20, there was no evidence to indicate that there was any misconduct inattention to duty, incompetency or willful violation of law or regulation regarding this casualty on the part of persons licensed or certificated by the Coast Guard.

17. No personnel of the Coast Guard, other agency of the Government or any other person either caused or contributed to the cause of the casualty or to the loss of life as a result thereof.

18. The evidence indicates that it is a practice for some Great Lakes ship masters to intentionally put water in their cargo holds in adverse weather in the belief that it will not only make their vessel ride better but will make it more stable. There is an apparent lack of knowledge of the reduction of stability caused by free surface effect.

19. It could not be determined whether the general alarm or other means of communications alerted all persons in the after section of the vessel. There was sufficient time before the sinking for all persons aft to be informed. It is unknown whether any persons were actually trapped inside the vessel at the time of sinking.

20. Although the requirements of the Federal Regulations were met, the general alarm system as installed is susceptible to improvement. There was no method for activating the system aft once the lines leading forward were parted.

21. Although the cause of death of the three persons on the raft with Hale was listed as drowning, they probably drowned from their own body fluids, or mucus, since they were still on the liferafts and all were believed to be conscious until immediately prior to death.

22. Although the lifeboat davits were not cranked out, the after crew might have removed the gripes. It is also considered possible that the force of water might have broken them loose. It could not be determined what happened to the port lifeboat as it was never located. However, it could have sustained damages from the fallen after mast or the air tanks could have been crushed by water pressure.

23. All persons who are missing or known dead probably lost their lives before the Coast Guard was informed that the DANIEL J. MORRELL was overdue. A positive vessel reporting procedure is considered highly desirable.

24. There were leaking rivets in some of the DANIEL J. MORRELL's side tanks upon arrival in Toledo, Ohio for winter lay up in 1965. The tanks causing most concern were the numbers 4 and 5 port side tanks. Vessel personnel entered tanks 4 and 5 port and marked leaking rivets with paint prior to lay up. The exact number of leaks could not be determined, as estimates ranged from no more than 12 to a maximum of 500 leaky rivets. It is held that the actual number was much closer to the lower estimate. The statements by Mr. Harvey Hays that he assisted in marking up to 500 leaking rivets in side tanks and of Dennis N. Hale that he observed approximately 1000 rivets marked for repairs on the hull of the vessel above the side tank top level is not sufficiently reliable to support a finding of fact. The probability does exist, however, that Mr. Hays did actually enter side tanks with another person and marked a small number of leaking rivets. Support for the rejection of the above statements is that trained inspectors, surveyors and company personnel did not observe the supposedly marked rivets during the 1965 lay up season. It is possible that markings of side tank rivets were obliterated at the

time that inspections were made. That the leaking into the port side tanks had been stopped or reduced and that Captain Hull was satisfied that the rivet problem had been corrected in drydock is accepted as fact. It is reasonable to assume that had there been any unusual leaking into side tanks or alarm over the condition of shell rivets, subsequent to his assuming command, Capt. Crawley would have reported this fact to company officials. There is no evidence to substantiate any inference that leaky or faulty rivets caused or contributed to the cause of the casualty.

25. The forecast issued by the U. S. Weather Bureau for the southern two-thirds of Lake Huron at 1200 EST, 28 November 1966 to cover the ensuing eighteen hour period was not sufficient to cause apprehension on the part of shipmasters. Vessels could generally expect protection in the lee of the Michigan shore. The weather information broadcast at 1800, which forecast winds of gale force from the north, was not interpreted by vessel masters as presenting conditions clearly dangerous to their operations. For this reason, most of the upbound vessels located in the Port Huron-Harbor Beach area continued northward until the wind force and action of the seas turned them around and forced their return to refuge in the Port Huron area. The winds were somewhat stronger and were from different directions than those expected. The sea conditions were much worse than would ordinarily be anticipated with the existing winds.

Whether a ship should or should not proceed in heavy weather conditions is a command decision. There is no clear showing that either the master of the SS DANIEL J. MORRELL or the masters of the other vessels who proceeded into the face of the storm were negligent for doing so.

26. The procedure of preparing forecasts every 6 hours does not in itself give sufficient advance warning to mariners since the seas build up so rapidly on the Great Lakes. It is believed that actual sea condition reports and sea condition

forecasts issued by the U. S. Weather Bureau would contribute to the safety of vessels transiting the Great Lakes.

27. There was no evidence to indicate the reboilering, repowering, or vessel alterations since initial construction either caused or contributed to the cause of the casualty. No evidence was received to support a finding that previous loading, unloading or ballasting procedures contributed to the casualty.

28. Based on estimated positions of vessels in the area, the radar target observed by the master of the BENSON FORD between 0100 and 0130 off the starboard beam was probably the EDWARD Y. TOWNSEND.

29. Had the two screen bulkheads located in the cargo holds been of watertight construction, it is possible that one or both sections of the vessel would have remained afloat.

30. Loading manuals are not as a rule furnished to masters of Great Lakes bulk carriers and consequently masters cannot readily determine the effect of a particular loading or ballasting condition upon longitudinal bending moments. In the instant case it is felt that there was a shift in the normal loading pattern of the ballast caused by leakage from the ballast tanks and this effect was probably unknown to Captain Crawley. This effect is indeterminate because it is not clear whether the ballast tanks were refilled periodically to replenish the water which had leaked into the holds.

RECOMMENDATIONS

Based on the foregoing, it is recommended that:

1. The required forward and after life rafts on Great Lakes vessels be of the inflatable type to provide for easy launching and protection of personnel against the weather.

2. The capacity of the forward and after life rafts be sufficient to provide protection for all persons normally quartered in each part of the vessel.

3. To improve reliability of radio communication under conditions where the connection with the source of power aft is severed, that:

    a. The Federal Regulations be changed to require an emergency source of power forward on Great Lakes vessels which have berthing and/or working spaces located both forward and aft, or

    b. That consideration be given to recommending to the Federal Communications Commission, Washington, D. C. that an emergency radio with a self-contained source of power be required, and

    c. That there be provided a datum marker buoy with the capacity of transmitting on 2182 kc. and capable of being either manually activated or automatically released and activated at a predetermined depth upon the sinking of the vessel. This could be stored with one of the required life rafts or attached with a pressure-release device to the side of the pilot house.

4. Special examinations of the hull structures of all Great Lakes vessels built prior to 1948 be conducted in order that a determination might be made as to whether weaknesses in hull plating or supporting structure have developed since the date of construction. NOTE: New ship steel specifications were adopted in 1948.

5. The owner or operator of each Great Lakes Bulk Carrier be required to furnish the Master a loading manual which shows the effect of various loaded and ballasted conditions upon longitudinal bending moments. The effects of dynamic forces of free water in cargo holds should be included.

6. Consideration be given to change 46 CFR 113.25 to provide, for typical Great Lakes bulk carriers, regardless of date of construction, which have manned spaces separated by cargo holds, that:

    a. The general alarm system shall be operated by means of manually operated contact makers located in the wheelhouse and in the engine room or at another suitable location in the after section of the vessel.

    b. A separate source of power for the general alarm system be installed in the circuit at each end of the vessel and the installation be made so that if the circuit be broken the forward alarms and the after alarms may be operated independently.

7. Further evaluation be made of the necessity to install tarpaulins over sliding plate type hatch covers which are properly secured, to determine whether or not the Master of a Great Lakes vessel may be authorized by regulation to sail without tarpaulins in place during all seasons when the vessel is not carrying cargo.

8. Vessel owners and operators be encouraged to initiate a positive vessel reporting system. Reports at 24 hour intervals would be desirable. If the vessel does not report within one hour of the scheduled time the company should take positive action to determine the status of the vessel.

9. Consideration be given to requiring cargo hold compartmentation on newly constructed Great Lakes vessels so that in the event any one main cargo hold should be flooded the vessel will have sufficient buoyancy to remain afloat.

10. A recommendation be made to the U. S. Weather Bureau that some system be instituted to make possible the inclusion of on scene and forecasted sea conditions into regular marine weather broadcasts.

11. Since the screw joining the two major component groups of many signal pistols is not installed to prevent its working loose and dropping out, it is recommended that 46 CFR 160.028 be revised to require that when such screws are installed there be provision, such as use of lock nuts or peening of the ends, to prevent the screw from backing out.

12. The Master of the SS DANIEL J. MORRELL, Arthur I. Crawley, being deceased, it is recommended that no action be taken regarding his omitting the use of tarpaulins over the sliding plate hatch covers.

CHARLES TIGHE
Rear Admiral, U. S. Coast Guard
Chairman

W. A. BRUSO
Captain, U. S. Coast Guard
Member

ROBERT P. CHIRNSIDE
Commander, U. S. Coast Guard
Member

WILFRED R. BLEAKLEY, Jr.
Commander, U. S. Coast Guard
Member

RICHARD J. AKRIDGE
Lieutenant, U. S. Coast Guard
Member and Recorder

SOURCES AND ACKNOWLEDGMENTS

Many years have passed since the loss of the Daniel J. Morrell in 1966, so re-creating the sinking of the vessel and Dennis Hale's remarkable survival involved a prodigious amount of research that included reading published books, newspaper articles, and magazine accounts about the sinking; interviewing Hale and others; and finding photographs that might add texture to my written text. I am grateful for all the help I received along the way.

First and foremost, I thank Dennis Hale, the shipwreck's only survivor. One cannot hear his riveting story without being deeply moved by the way the Morrell tragedy affected his life. That he survived is nothing less than incredible, but that is only one aspect of the story. That he lived through the ups and downs of the years after the sinking, battling his own physical issues and psychological demons, represents a division of self as real as the Morrell's splitting in two on the surface of Lake Huron.

Hale's two books about the Morrell—Sole Survivor, with Tim Juhl and Pat and Jim Stayer (1996), and Shipwrecked (2010)—were essential for my research, as well as good readings. Hale passed away in 2015, before he had the chance to see this book fully realized.

Besides Hale's written accounts, I consulted other books in my research. Andrew Kantar's Deadly Voyage, a brief but outstanding account of the sinking and its aftermath, was a valuable place to start, as was William Ratigan's classic Great Lakes Shipwrecks and Survivals, an overview of many of the disasters on these five bodies of water. Walter Havighurst's The Long Ships Passing remains the finest history of early Great Lakes shipping I have read.

I am pleased to call Mark L. Thompson, author, former Great Lakes sailor, and valued historian, a friend and go-to research source. His book Graveyard of the Lakes rivals Ratigan's for its concise look at a number of shipwrecks, and his Steamboats and Sailors of the Great Lakes and Queen of the Lakes are essential introductions to Great Lakes shipping history. A Sailor's

Logbook, his diary of a season on the lakes, is both informative and a pleasure to read.

I read hundreds of newspaper and magazine pieces, and they assisted me immensely in the pacing of this book. The day-to-day newspaper accounts, especially those published by papers around Lake Huron, were both immediate and suspenseful, and many offered daily coverage of the Coast Guard hearings. I can't begin to name each newspaper here, but those of particular value include the *Benton Harbor (Mich.) News-Palladium*, the *Escanaba (Mich.) Daily Press*, the *Holland (Mich.) Evening Sentinel*, the *Ironwood (Mich.) Daily Globe*, the *Ludington (Mich.) Daily News*, the *Port Huron (Mich.) Times Herald*, the *Sault Ste. Marie (Mich.) Evening News*, and the *Traverse City (Mich.) Record Eagle*.

Marine Casualty Report: S.S. Daniel J. Morrell, the Coast Guard's report on the findings of its board of inquiry, is the Holy Grail of *Daniel J. Morrell* narratives, packed with a timeline of the *Morrell*'s fateful trip, statistics and information about the boat and storm, and recommendations for improved safety in the future. It remains one of the most thorough reports of its kind that I have read. *Sinking of the SS Daniel J. Morrell in Lake Huron with Loss of Life*, the National Transportation Safety Board's written review of the Coast Guard report and recommendations based on that review, was also very useful.

Dr. Robert Oakes, the first physician to examine Dennis Hale after his rescue, offered a detailed description of Hale's medical condition and treatment. Almost as interesting were his observations about Hale's hallucinations and the importance they were to his survival.

Paul Nyren spoke of his experiences in helping with the search and rescue communications from his Coast Guard post in Northbrook, Illinois.

Roland Schultz, quartermaster on the Coast Guard cutter *Bramble* at the time of the storm, gave me extensive information on the search for survivors or victims of the *Morrell* and on the successful search for the boat's wrecked stern section.

Captain Chuck Millradt, commander of the Coast Guard cutter *Acacia* during the search and rescue operations for the *Morrell*, shared his memories of those difficult days. Dennis Miller, a Coast Guard electrician onboard the *Acacia* during the storm and its aftermath, also shared his experiences in the storm and subsequent search for victims and survivors of the *Daniel J. Morrell*. Art Lind, onboard the *Mackinaw* during the storm, recalled his experiences in the *Nordmeer* rescue operation as well as the search and rescue mission for the *Morrell*. Lonnie Mixon, an operations officer at the Coast Guard's Detroit Air Station, offered an account of his participation in the helicopter rescue of the eight crew members of the *Nordmeer* and of his efforts in the search and rescue operations for the *Morrell*.

Great Lakes explorer and shipwreck hunter David Trotter offered me a compelling account of his discovery of the *Morrell*'s bow section.

I owe a debt of gratitude to my friend Greg Bonofiglio, who once again came up with numerous research sources that added depth to the narrative. His eye for detail and ability to use it for further analysis were very helpful.

Thanks, too, to those who always seem to be around when I need them: Al and Diane Schumacher, Susan Schumacher, Ken Ade, the group at Franks Diner, and my brothers and sisters.

My thanks to the staff at the University of Minnesota Press, in particular to my editor, Erik Anderson, and his assistant, Kristian Tvedten.

And finally, Adam, Emily Joy, and Jack Henry: all my love.

INDEX

Michael Schumacher is the author of fifteen books. His three books about the Great Lakes include *Mighty Fitz* (Minnesota, 2012), an account of the sinking of the *Edmund Fitzgerald*; *Wreck of the Carl D.*, the story of the loss of the *Carl D. Bradley*; and *November's Fury* (Minnesota, 2013), an account of the Great Lakes Storm of 1913. He lives in Wisconsin, near the shores of Lake Michigan.